Interactive Writing

Students and Teachers "Sharing the Pen" to Create Meaningful Text

Written by
Trisha Callella and Kimberly Jordano

Editor
Kristine Johnson

Illustrator
Darcy Tom

Cover Photographer
Michael Jarrett

Designer
Carmela Burgos

Cover Designer
Barbara Peterson

Art Director
Tom Cochrane

Project Director
Carolea Williams

CTP © 2000 Creative Teaching Press, Inc., Huntington Beach, CA 92649

Table of Contents

Introduction

Interactive writing is a teacher-guided group activity designed to teach children about the process of writing and how written language works. During interactive writing, children and their teacher "share the pen" to create meaningful text. They take turns writing the text together one word or letter at a time. Interactive writing may be about anything from news of the day to a letter, shopping list, or retelling of a familiar story. During interactive writing, children become more aware of the details of letters, sounds, and words while working together with their teacher to write a text that is significant to them. This supportive, dynamic environment helps children focus on the construction of their message while feeling successful and involved.

Interactive Writing contains simple directions for incorporating the interactive writing process into your literacy program. You will find tips and techniques for teaching interactive writing, sample interactive writing lessons, ideas for using suggested interactive writing resources, an assessment, and writing activities that include all children—from emergent to developing and more advanced reading levels. The interactive writing activities provide the content to which the interactive writing method is applied. They provide fun formats and topics for conducting interactive writing that encompass language arts, social studies, science, and math. The activities are arranged by curriculum area so you can incorporate interactive writing throughout your day. Each activity has an extension idea that features a component from a balanced literacy program. *Interactive Writing* will help you give the children in your classroom skills and strategies to use and control the conventions of written language.

We went on a nature walk to

What Is Interactive Writing?

Interactive writing is a method of writing during which the teacher and child write meaningful text together. This process builds upon what children have learned from language experience (dictation) and shared writing and increases class participation in the act of writing. To begin interactive writing, the teacher gathers children around an easel so they all can see the writing and can quickly come up to the easel to write. The teacher and children create a message or text. Examples of appropriate writing include a description of something the children have learned or seen, labels for a story map or mural, a story, a letter, directions, a list, or any of the activity suggestions found on pages 34–73. Then, individual children come to the easel and write individual letters, groups of letters (word chunks), words they know, or punctuation. The teacher and children say each word slowly to listen for all the sounds in each word. The teacher oversees the work, guiding them and interacting with them, and fills in what is unknown.

In the interactive writing process, every child is given the opportunity to apply what he or she knows about language and build on that prior knowledge. Children take an active role in the writing process as the teacher scaffolds the learning. Scaffolding is a teaching technique that includes responsive conversation, open-ended questions, and encouragement for children to verbalize their thinking. Scaffolding provides children with verbal assistance and promotes discovery based on the child's level of sophistication. The teacher focuses the children's attention on the sounds and spellings of words and the conventions of print, such as spaces between words, left-to-right and top-to-bottom directionality, capital letters, and punctuation. Whether children are simply providing the space between words, writing the beginning blend in a word, or writing entire words, they are active participants in the writing process.

Since text created during interactive writing is intended to be read again and again, and since the teacher is at hand overseeing the work, all text should adhere to standard conventions of spelling and grammar. This will help children in their understanding of the processes involved in spelling. Interactive writing is an ideal time to teach not only correct spelling and concepts about print, but to introduce correct letter formation, teach the use of punctuation, develop phonics skills, and increase reading fluency while writing meaningful text. It is a powerful tool in teaching children to read and write.

Stages of Interactive Writing

The characteristics of interactive writing change as children become more proficient readers and writers. Since the end product of interactive writing will be used for rereading, all letters and conventions of print need to be accurate and legible. This includes proper letter formation, use of capital letters, punctuation, and spaces between words. During interactive writing, there are numerous opportunities to teach different skills and strategies. Reading by children and teacher with phrasing and fluency should begin on day one. This is why rereading the text as it is written and when it is finished is so important at all stages of interactive writing. The reading should not sound choppy, but should flow like conversation. This section outlines the features of interactive writing during the emergent, developing, and advanced stages and presents tips for each stage.

Emergent Stage

In the emergent stage, interactive writing may consist of modeling letter formation on a dry-erase board or magnetic writing board (e.g., MagnaDoodle®). The teacher may even need to hold a child's hand to help him or her write the correct letter. The child may want to practice writing the letter on the dry-erase board or MagnaDoodle before writing it on the easel. At this stage, the teacher assists the children in segmenting words to hear and record individual sounds. Children are typically writing one letter at a time. They are practicing sound-letter relationships. Children can contribute a letter of a word when their name has the same first letter. For example, Bailey could write the *b* in *bus* and Samantha could add the *s*. Some children can serve as "spacers," by placing two fingers between words to establish spacing. Others may add punctuation. Later on, they will advance to writing blends and whole words, rather than individual letters. Start by spending no more than 15 minutes on interactive writing with young children. As the year progresses, lessons can last 20 to 30 minutes.

Through interactive writing, you can demonstrate and engage children in every aspect of the writing process. During the emergent stage of interactive writing, keep in mind the following suggestions:

- Ensure all text is student-generated.
- Keep the text short.
- Have children sit close to the writing area.
- Model correct letter formation on a dry-erase board or MagnaDoodle.
- Invite children to practice writing their contribution on a dry-erase board or MagnaDoodle before writing on the easel.
- For students who need extra help, write a letter or word in pencil, and have them trace it in marker.
- Model phoneme segmentation.
- Teach these concepts about print:
  - Address how text is written and read in a left-to-right progression.
  - Count the number of words in a sentence.
  - Point out the spaces between words.
  - Capitalize the first letter of a sentence.
  - Teach the correct usage of ending punctuation (e.g., period, question mark, exclamation point).
  - Explain the difference between a letter and a word.
  - Discuss return sweep.

- Edit spelling using magic "fix-it" tape (correction tape or white mailing labels).
- Maximize children's involvement by having them clap syllables of new words and use their hands to "stretch" each word.
- Give alliterative praise when children write individual letters, such as "super s's," "terrific t's," and "outrageous o's. This helps children feel proud of their contribution and gives extra phonemic awareness practice.
- Choose a child to be the spacer whenever a space is needed between words. This will especially benefit children who are just beginning to develop concepts about print. They feel like they have made a contribution. All children feel successful, and every child is a writer.
- Have children count the words and jump up for each word.
- Reread the text before adding each new word.
- For longer messages, write one sentence (or one word) at each sitting. Reread previous sentences before composing new ones.
- Model fluency and expression.
- Have children rehearse the sentence so they remember it. Invite them to tell the sentence to their neighbors and then whisper it to you. Invite children to also "tell" their knees, elbows, feet, etc.

Emergent Stage

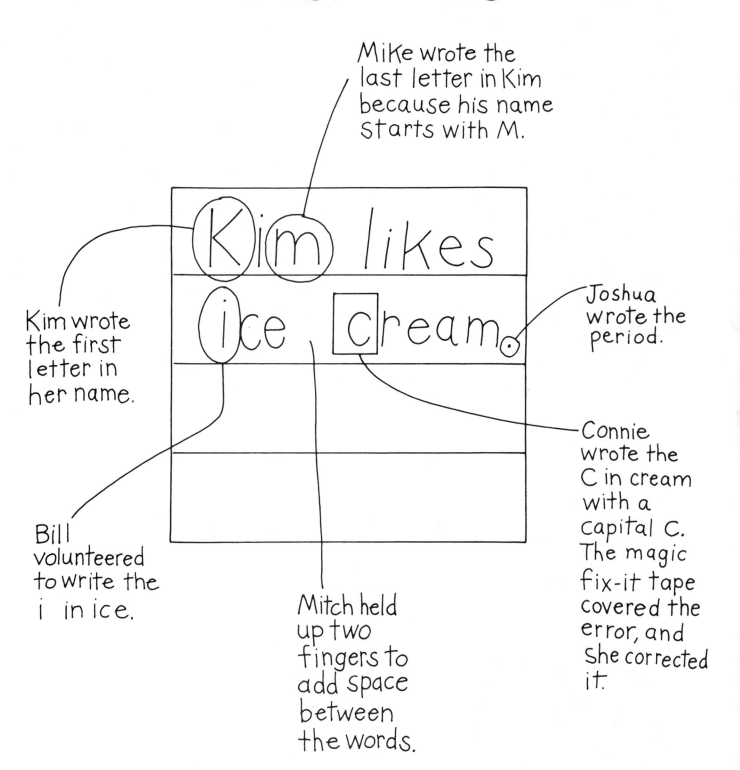

Mike wrote the last letter in Kim because his name starts with M.

Kim wrote the first letter in her name.

Bill volunteered to write the i in ice.

Mitch held up two fingers to add space between the words.

Joshua wrote the period.

Connie wrote the C in cream with a capital C. The magic fix-it tape covered the error, and she corrected it.

Kim likes ice cream.

Developing Stage

As children develop their writing skills, they begin to record blends, "chunks" (parts of words), and whole words (high-frequency words and known words). During the developing stage, they use known words to write unknown but similar words. For example, if a sentence contains the unknown word *let*, the teacher could say *You know* get, *so you can spell* let. This teaches children to make analogies. Children in the developing stage are ready as a group to write more than one sentence during the interactive writing process.

During each interactive writing session, choose different children to be the "recorders." These children write the sentences on individual dry-erase boards as other children are interactively writing. When the sentences are complete, the recorders show their writing. (This is a great opportunity for you to assess the recorders' ability to write sentences.) At this stage, children will be writing the high-frequency words they have learned and those that are on the word wall.

Because they are rereading text they have written, children learn to read with proper phrasing and fluency. Rereading also provides opportunities to teach reading strategies. For example, say *Does it make sense? Does it sound right? Does it look right?* or *Look for little words in big words.*

During the developing stage, keep in mind the following:

- Aid children in phoneme segmentation.
- Focus on beginning blends.
- Have children divide words into chunks and word families.
- Reinforce correct letter formation.
- Edit spelling using magic fix-it tape.
- Reread text with children before adding each new word.
- Address how to form plurals.
- Teach phonics patterns, such as how silent *e* changes a short vowel to a long one.
- Use correct punctuation, including the introduction of the comma and quotation marks.
- Include polysyllabic words.
- Discuss compound words.

Stages of Interactive Writing

Developing Stage

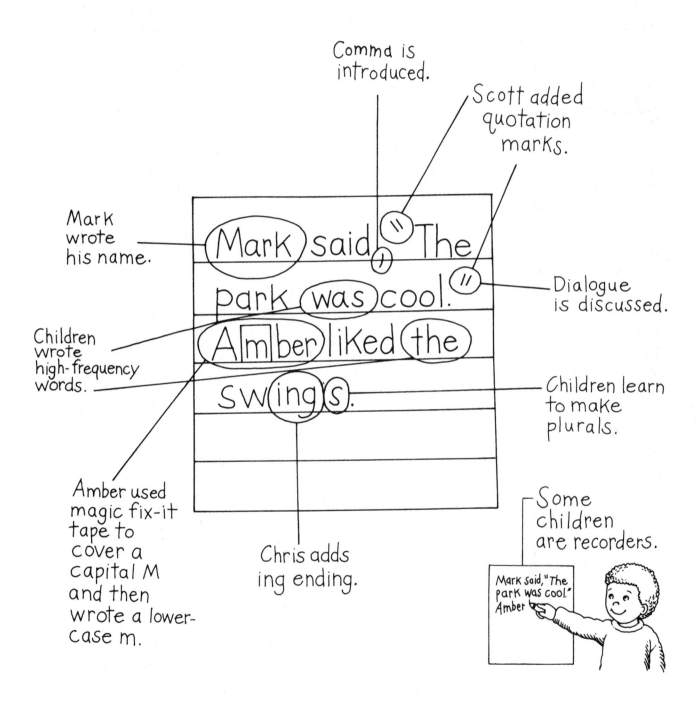

Comma is introduced.

Scott added quotation marks.

Mark wrote his name.

Dialogue is discussed.

Children wrote high-frequency words.

Children learn to make plurals.

Amber used magic fix-it tape to cover a capital M and then wrote a lower-case m.

Chris adds ing ending.

Some children are recorders.

Mark said, "The park was cool." Amber

Mark said, "The park was cool. Amber liked the swings.

Advanced Stage

During interactive writing with more advanced children, draw attention to word patterns and make connections between words. Since the writing is student-generated, the text will not be composed to illustrate spelling patterns. But as children are able to compose longer and more complex sentences, many examples emerge to help teach children more about words. Help children create sentences that are descriptive, and recognize opportunities to teach concepts and principles from the children's writing. To save time, write the words that children already know without their help so you can concentrate on the skills you are trying to teach them.

During the advanced stage of interactive writing, keep in mind the following:

- Have all children act as recorders at this stage. Have them record the interactive writing message on dry-erase boards or interactive writing paper (page 74). Combine the paper into books for rereading.
- Have children write several high-frequency words and use segmentation, chunking, and knowledge of word families to spell unknown words.
- Stay on the cutting edge of the children's learning. Supply the easy parts and known words, such as *a, the, to, in,* and *it,* so children will focus on the actual learning at their level of development.
- Help children link words. For example, to write the word *bright,* say *You know* night, *so you can write* bright.
- Help children learn how to segment and record sounds in compound and polysyllabic words.
- Teach correct spelling and sentence structure.
- Reinforce letter formation.
- Focus on blends and digraphs.
- Divide words into chunks and word families.
- Include descriptive writing.
- Include informational text writing.
- Have children discuss the elements of a story.
- Invite children to retell stories.
- Use more sophisticated punctuation, including the hyphen and apostrophe.
- Teach contractions.

Advanced Stage

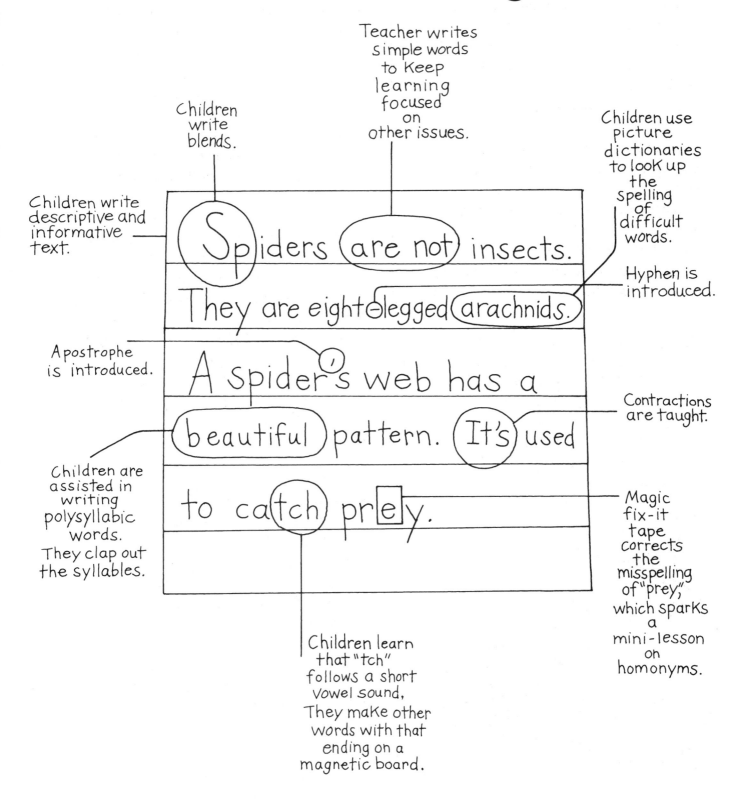

Teacher writes simple words to keep learning focused on other issues.

Children write blends.

Children use picture dictionaries to look up the spelling of difficult words.

Children write descriptive and informative text.

Hyphen is introduced.

Apostrophe is introduced.

Contractions are taught.

Children are assisted in writing polysyllabic words. They clap out the syllables.

Magic fix-it tape corrects the misspelling of "prey," which sparks a mini-lesson on homonyms.

Children learn that "tch" follows a short vowel sound. They make other words with that ending on a magnetic board.

Spiders are not insects.

They are eight-legged arachnids.

A spider's web has a beautiful pattern. It's used

to catch prey.

A Balanced Literacy Program

In addition to interactive writing, the following elements of reading and writing ought to be a part of every balanced literacy program. Each activity in this book contains an extension related to one of the components of a balanced literacy program. The following section describes each component and lists its most important benefits.

Modeled Reading

Teacher read-alouds are opportunities for modeled reading. During modeled reading, the teacher and children engage in meaningful conversation about the ideas in the book. Children make predictions about the story and comment about the characters and main events. The teacher models the joy of reading and uses correct phrasing and expressive fluency. Modeled reading

- fosters a love and enthusiasm for reading
- exposes children to a variety of genres
- develops knowledge of the structure of language
- enriches concept and vocabulary development
- puts children in touch with their emotions in a nonthreatening way

Shared Reading

During shared reading, the teacher and children read in unison from the same enlarged-print book, song, or poem. Shared reading enables the teacher to teach skills and reading strategies within the context of a story. Group problem solving occurs during shared reading, as there is conversation about the story such as predicting, reading of familiar phrases, recognition of repeated and new words, and reading of character names. Shared reading

- encourages children to participate and "bond" with the book
- increases children's ability to find known and unknown words within a text
- allows children to connect stories to background experiences, make predictions, and retell stories
- expands children's vocabulary
- promotes independent reading

Guided Reading

During guided reading, the teacher works with children who are grouped according to ability level. The children independently and quietly read the same simple story or one that has been part of several shared reading experiences so they will have successful experiences reading without frustration. Guided reading

- allows children to view themselves as readers
- gives each child an opportunity to apply learning from shared reading and interactive writing experiences
- encourages children to engage in conversation by asking questions and sharing information that they notice about the text
- builds self-confidence
- allows the teacher to work briefly with individual students as they need it
- provides an opportunity for children to practice using cueing systems so they can maintain comprehension while they read increasingly difficult levels of text
- strengthens children's thinking skills

Independent Reading

During independent reading, children individually read materials ranging from simple books and charts to increasingly difficult stories as reading skills grow. Independent reading is for practice and enjoyment. Independent reading

- helps children read for meaning
- allows children to solve difficulties using good reading strategies
- is self-paced and self-programmed
- allows children to take responsibility for their own learning
- establishes good reading habits
- promotes fluency and challenges children to become independent problem solvers

Language Experience

The language experience approach entails individual children dictating text while the teacher records it. Children's own experiences stimulate conversation and writing. The teacher demonstrates forming letters, constructing words and sentences, and using writing conventions and correct punctuation. Language experience

- allows children to see their words in print and the forming of words and sentences
- models that spoken words can be written down and print can be read aloud
- gives children ownership of the written material
- provides an avenue to more sophisticated language because the text is based on the children's oral language, not necessarily text they could write on their own
- motivates children to reread the text

Modeled Writing

During modeled writing, the teacher writes a message, such as daily news, morning message, center directions, a daily schedule, or a note to the class, in front of the children. The teacher thinks aloud while writing to the class, modeling capital letters, letter/sound relationship, letter formation, punctuation, and completeness of thought. The teacher draws attention to rhyming words, sequence of events, and familiar words. Modeled writing

- shows children that writing serves a purpose
- allows children to see writing modeled for them

Shared Writing

Shared writing involves the teacher recording ideas shared by the children and guides the process so the text is highly readable for them. Shared writing encourages children to share ideas as the teacher asks questions to clarify the meaning and talks with them about the purpose of the writing and its intended audience. The teacher, acting as scribe, writes the collaborated message. Shared writing

- demonstrates "mental modeling" (i.e., the teacher thinks aloud about the writing process, concepts about print, and conventions of print)
- offers frequent opportunities to read and reread the text
- builds self-confidence

Guided Writing

During guided writing, the teacher works with a group of children similar in strengths and needs and provides instruction through mini-lessons. The teacher offers children choices about what to write through conferences and sharing circles. Guided writing

- models brainstorming of ideas
- provides children with the guidance they need to learn the writing process and produce high-quality writing
- provides an audience for the written word

Independent Writing

Independent writing includes all writing children do with minimal support. Independent writing

- provides opportunities for open-ended writing experiences, such as writing letters, making invitations, journal writing, creative writing, and making lists
- helps children learn to use strategies that have been introduced during previous writing experiences

Preparing for Interactive Writing

Conduct interactive writing in a central part of your room where all children can see the writing as it takes place. Choose an easel that can be easily seen and written on by all the children. Use dark-colored markers so the children can easily see the writing. When beginning the interactive writing process, use a different-colored dark marker for each word to help children notice the difference between words and track print.

To ensure that every child is successful, establish a nonthreatening environment. Choose children to contribute to the writing based on their background knowledge. For example, ask children to write a letter they know because it is in their name. Create a forgiving environment. For example, when writing the sentence *Today we will eat pizza,* a child may write the numeral 2 in an attempt to begin the word *Today.* Use this as a "teachable moment" by introducing magic fix-it tape—correction tape or white mailing labels that cover mistakes, or learning opportunities, made by the children. Be sure to use the tape to correct your own errors to model that everyone makes mistakes. Taking part in a forgiving learning environment teaches children that mistakes are acceptable.

To begin interactive writing, gather a variety of classroom materials. Activities in this book refer to "interactive writing materials," which include items such as the following:

Reference Materials
Select current and easy-to-use classroom reference books. Since interactive writing always includes correct spelling and often includes informational text, picture dictionaries, a children's encyclopedia, a rhyming dictionary, and a children's thesaurus are useful resources to have.

Name Chart

Create a wall display with children's names on it. Or, write each child's name on a sentence strip, glue his or her class photo to the end, and store these name cards in a pocket chart. One of the first things a child learns to write is his or her name, so using children's names during interactive writing is an effective way to develop letter knowledge.

Alex M.	Cody	Sam
Alex J.	Cassie	Sid
Andre	Jenna	Sarah
Ashley	Jasmine	Taylor
Brooke	Luke	Travis
Bryan	Nathan	Vicky
Bradley	Riley	

Alphabet Chart

Post an alphabet chart near the interactive writing area for children's reference. Display a chart that has uppercase and lowercase letters and a picture beginning with each letter's sound.

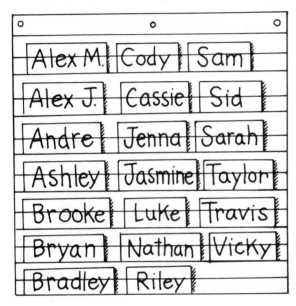

Easel

An easel is the focal point of any interactive writing lesson. Have all the children seated so they can see the easel and easily come up to write on it. Display chart paper, sentence strips, or large writing paper on the easel.

Word Wall

Choose a place in your classroom to display high-frequency words. Create space for words beginning with each letter of the alphabet. As children learn high-frequency words, add them to the word wall. Word walls help children develop a supply of words for writing. Reserve the word wall for only familiar words that you want the children to learn to spell correctly. Always try to incorporate as many high-frequency words as possible to maximize children's opportunities for reading, writing, and spelling these words.

Butcher Paper

Create large writing surfaces from butcher paper in the shape of objects that the children write about. For example, cut out a rabbit gardener from butcher paper when recording favorite vegetables. Have children write on sentence strips or cash-register tape so mistakes can be covered up with magic fix-it tape on the white paper instead of directly on the colored butcher paper. The strips also help guide children to write letters and words that are proportionate in size.

Chart Paper

Place chart paper on an easel during interactive writing. Children can begin the interactive writing process on unlined paper. Later, add lines to help guide children in their letter formation and sizing.

Large Writing Paper

As children become more skilled in writing letters, they will improve their letter formation by practicing on lined writing paper. Guide children so they write their letters within a given area.

Interactive Writing Paper

Have individual children who are more advanced in their writing copy the interactive writing text onto their own interactive writing paper (see page 74). This will keep those children focused on the writing and also give them extra writing practice. Have the children take the paper home and reread it to their families.

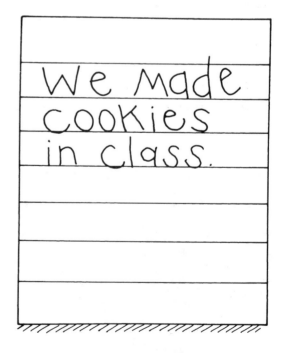

Monthly Word Bank

Display a chart with words that are appropriate to the month or season. For example, October's word bank might be in the shape of a pumpkin and contain words such as *pumpkin, bat,* and *spider.* When seasonal words come up in reading or class discussions, add them to the word bank for use in interactive writing lessons.

Magic Fix-It Tape

Magic fix-it tape is simply white correction tape or white mailing labels. Use it to show children that mistakes are learning opportunities. For example, if a child writes an *s* backwards, say *That's all right. We can fix it with the magic fix-it tape!* Then, invite the child to put a piece of tape or a white label on top of the mistake and write over it. Since interactive writing text will be reread many times in the classroom, the text needs to be spelled correctly. Use the magic fix-it tape for all corrections. You will use a ton of it in the beginning. Have a generous supply on hand!

Magnetic Letters

Magnetic letters can be used for linking known words to unknown words or for generating word families. Put several magnetic letters on a metal surface to play "Make It, Break It." Spell a simple word, such as *cat.* Then, mix up the letters, and ask a child to put them back together. Have children spell other known words with the magnetic letters. Compare them to similar unknown words. Ask children to explain how they are similar. For example, *big* and *wig* both end with the same sound. Have children use the magnetic letters to create other words in the same word family. To demonstrate how little words are sometimes found in bigger words, use magnetic letters to spell *Wednesday,* and have the children locate the words *we* and *day* within the word. Cover a popcorn tin with contact paper. Store the letters in the tin, and have children make words on the outside.

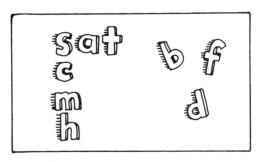

Magnetic Writing Board

A magnetic writing board (MagnaDoodle) is wonderful for children to use while writing. Children can write on it during interactive writing and then rewrite mistakes without a trace of the correction.

Dry-Erase Boards

A large dry-erase board is great to use for interactive writing, and a class set of dry-erase boards allows each child to copy the interactive writing text while a classmate writes it on the easel. Individual dry-erase boards can be purchased inexpensively at a local home improvement store. Ask for melamine board to be cut into 9" x 12" (23 cm x 30.5 cm) rectangles.

Dry-Erase Markers

Since dry-erase markers are used so often during interactive writing, ask for parents to donate them. Store the markers tip side down for maximum longevity.

Erasers

Not only are old socks perfect erasers for dry-erase markers, they are perfect containers for them, too! Or, glue felt to small wooden blocks to make erasers. This is a good parent volunteer job. When all else fails, give each child a tissue.

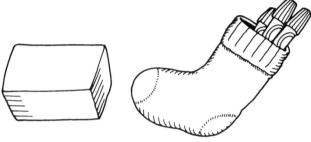

Cash-Register Tape

Cash-register tape is easy to use and can be purchased at an office supply store. Place the tape over unlined chart paper to create visual lines for children to write on. The white cash-register tape also prevents the magic fix-it tape from showing up when the writing background is on colored butcher paper.

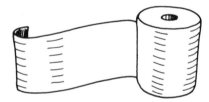

Sentence Strips

Pocket chart sentence strips work well for children to write on in lieu of the cash-register tape. The lines help guide them in their letter formation and sizing, and the neutral color does not show magic fix-it tape corrections. As a less expensive alternative, photocopy sentence strips and glue the photocopy to chart or butcher paper.

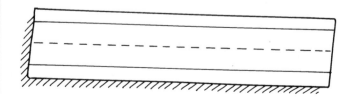

Colored Markers

Use dark-colored markers for writing on sentence strips, cash-register tape, or chart paper so the words can be easily read from a distance. Have children use different-colored markers for each word so they can easily see the words and differentiate one word from the next. Scented markers are extra fun!

Spacing Sticks

Tongue depressors and craft sticks make great spacing tools. Children enjoy decorating their own spacer with sequin and bead "jewels" and paint. Spacers allow the children's writing hand to be free as they write. (Sometimes children have trouble putting two fingers down or deciding which hand to use.)

Magic Reading Glasses

Punch out the lenses of old glasses, and add ribbon to the sides to make magic reading glasses. These are fun for children to wear during "Read the Room" time. This is when children look around the room with a partner and read anything around them, such as words on the word wall, poems on charts, a morning message, or class-made books.

Author's Chair

Make an Author's Chair from an inexpensive director's chair. Decorate the back with fabric paints. Invite children to sit in the chair while reading their writing to the class.

Photos

Use photos of children, the school environment, and staff during interactive writing. Show photos and ask the children to talk about or describe what is happening in the photos. The photos will help children create text that is important to them.

Wikki Stix®

Have children use Wikki Stix to locate, circle, or underline letters, word chunks, punctuation, or small words in bigger words. Wikki Stix work like wax-covered pipe cleaners and can be stuck to surfaces to frame words or word parts.

Tips and Techniques

The interactive writing *process* is more important than the product. To get and keep children interested during the process, keep the beginning interactive writing experiences upbeat, active, and fast paced. Otherwise, you will find children rolling around on the carpet looking for staples. (Really!) To keep all children actively engaged throughout the interactive writing process, employ the following tips and techniques:

- Repeat the sentence before writing it.
- Have children say the sentence to the sky, the door, the floor, and their neighbor.
- Have children say the sentence in a different voice, such as a whisper, robot voice, loud voice, or scary voice.
- When repeating the sentence, have children snap or count with their fingers as they say each word.
- After counting words, have children repeat the sentence as you draw a line for each word. Repeat the sentence, demonstrating a one-to-one correspondence between words and spaces. Make the lines long enough to write the words on.
- When segmenting words to hear each sound, have children move their hands slowly apart as if stretching a rubber band.

- Before writing each new word, have children reread the words that have been written. Have a child use a pointer to track each word as it is read aloud, and invite the class to predict the next word.
- Allow children to become the spacers by having them put their fingers or spacing sticks on the page to mark the space between words.
- Write on a dry-erase board or with magnetic letters words children have already learned that are similar to new words they are writing. Help children make comparisons between the words.
- Help children generate word families when rhyming words occur in the sentence.
- When recording polysyllabic words, invite children to clap each syllable and then segment each syllable to hear and record the sounds.

Interactive Writing Prompts

Use the following sentences as a template to guide interactive writing. They are written in a sequential order that can be adapted for interactive writing with your class.

Emergent Stage

- *What do we want to say about _____?*
- *Let's say the sentence again. Say it to your _____.*
- *Let's count the words in our sentence with our fingers.*
- *What is the first word we will write?*
- *Say the word slowly. What is the first sound you hear?*
- *Who knows how to write the letter _____?*
- *Now, let's stretch the word like a rubber band.*
- *How many sounds do you hear?*
- *What sound do you hear next?*
- *Write the middle and last sounds.*
- *Let's read what we wrote.*
- *Does it look right?*
- *What word do we need to write next?*
- *Can you see/find that word anywhere in the classroom?*
- *What goes at the end of a sentence?*
- *What punctuation would you see at the end of a statement/question?*

Developing and Advanced Stages

- *What do we want to say about _____?*
- *Let's say the sentences again. Say them to your _____.*
- *Let's count the words in our first sentence with our fingers.*
- *What is our first word?*
- If a known word, *Who knows how to write the word _____?*
- If an unknown word, *Let's clap the word to hear how many syllables there are in _____.*
- If a word has a chunk, *Who knows what letters make this sound _____?* (e.g., *ight, un, eat, ch, ing*)
- *Who can write the sounds in the first part?*
- *Listen for the ending. What would sound right at the end?*
- *Does it look right?*
- *Add a letter to make it look right.*
- *Think about how the word looks. Do you know another word that looks like that?*
- *Let's read what we wrote.*
- *What word do we need to write next?*

Emergent Interactive Writing Sample

The following dialogue is an example of the process of writing a sentence using interactive writing.

Text: *We took a trip to the beach.*

Teacher: *The first word is* we. *Who knows how to write the word* we? *Where could we find that word in our room?*

Class: *It's on our calendar in the word Wednesday.* We.

Teacher: *Good.* Took. *We know the word* look, *so we can write the word* took. *Who wants to come up and write it? (Model* -ook *word family on a dry-erase board or with magnetic letters.) Let's point and read what we've written so far.*

Class: *We took*

Teacher: a. *We know how to write* a. *Who wants to come up and write it?*

Class: *We took a*

Teacher: trip. *Let's stretch the word* trip *like a rubber band. (Move hands apart as if stretching a rubber band.) What is the first sound you hear? (/tr/) Trevor, your name starts like that. Would you like to come up and write it for us? I'll write the ending. Say the word in slow motion.*

Class: *tr-i-p. We took a trip*

Teacher: to. *Who knows how to write the word* to? *(A child comes up and writes the numeral 2. Now you have a teachable moment.) You're right, that is a 2. That's the*

number two. *We need the word* to. *(Now you get to teach the word* to *the class. Write* to *and add it to the word wall. Use magic fix-it tape to cover the number, and let the same child write the word* to. *Thank the child for teaching the class.) What have we written now?*

Class: *We took a trip to*

Teacher: the. *Where can we find* the *in the classroom? Who wants to come write it?*

Class: *The is on our word wall. We took a trip to the*

Teacher: beach. *Let's stretch the word* beach *like a rubber band. (Move hands apart as if stretching a rubber band.) What do you hear at the beginning of* beeeeeeeach? *(Children might know the letter* b *or the word* be.) *There's a sneaky* a *in there that we can't hear. I'll write it for you. Let's stretch the word* beach *again. What do you hear at the end of* beeeeeach? *We have a friend in our class whose name starts like that. Who is it? Chandler! Would you like to come write the first two letters in your name? What's our sentence?*

Class: *We took a trip to the beach*

Teacher: *What punctuation belongs at the end of our sentence?*

Class: *A period.*

Teacher: *Who would like to put a period at the end of our sentence so we know where to stop and take a breath? (A child adds the period.)*

Class: *We took a trip to the beach.*

Advanced Interactive Writing Sample

The following shows the attention given to words in an example of interactive writing with a more advanced group of children.

Sample text: *We took a trip to the beach. We saw a spiky starfish. It looked bright purple in the freezing cold water.*

- Have the class repeat the text they want to write so they remember it. Have the class work on one sentence at a time.
- Have children independently write high-frequency words.
- Write very familiar words, such as *a, to, in, the,* and *it,* for the children to keep the pace of the lesson moving.
- Have children write the text on individual dry-erase boards or on paper while one child writes on an easel.
- Ask children to write words using chunks (e.g., *-ook, -ed, -ing, -ight, -er*) whenever possible.
- Have children clap the syllables of unknown words and then count the sounds in each part.

- Have children split compound words into syllables. After the word is written, cover each individual word and have children read each one separately.
- Write unheard vowels for the children (e.g., *a* in *beach*).
- Draw attention to silent letters, and ask children to check the word wall for other words with silent letters.
- Conduct mini-lessons on spelling patterns, such as *ar* in *starfish* or *ur* in *purple*. Make connections with the interactive writing text and other words that fit into that pattern.
- Add new words to word walls or monthly word banks.
- Let children contribute parts of the message that they can produce but still need to practice a bit more.
- Have children sort words under categories such as word families. Have children revisit the word sort several times and eventually make a wall chart to add more words in the future.

ar in st<u>ar</u>	
st<u>ar</u>fish	h<u>ar</u>p
st<u>ar</u>ch	ch<u>ar</u>t
l<u>ar</u>ge	sm<u>ar</u>t
sh<u>ar</u>k	sc<u>ar</u>
al<u>ar</u>m	m<u>ar</u>ch

A First Lesson

Use the following sample "script" as an example of a first interactive writing lesson.

Preparation

Take photographs of the children in your class or of the school. Glue each photo onto construction paper. Use tape or glue to attach a sentence strip or strip of cash-register tape under each picture. Gather the necessary materials from the recommended interactive writing resources listed on pages 16—21.

Process

1. Show the class the first photo you would like to use for interactive writing.
2. Discuss who or what is in the picture.
3. Guide children to create a simple three- to five-word sentence that describes the picture.
4. Have children repeat the sentence to neighbors, body parts, and the sky.
5. Have children count the words in the sentence with their fingers.
6. Point out on the strip approximately where each word would go or draw lines for the words as the sentence is repeated again.
7. Ask children if they think there is enough writing space for the sentence. If not, be ready to add more cash-register tape or another sentence strip.
8. Help children identify the first word of the sentence.
9. Help children segment the word and identify the first sound.
10. Choose a child whose name has that letter in it to come up and write that letter. Remind children that a sentence begins with a capital letter.
11. Model the correct letter formation on a dry-erase board or MagnaDoodle as the child writes the letter. Modeling will also help the writer feel successful. (Remember, the goal is for every child to feel successful and confident. Sometimes, you may need to take the child's hand for a "ride" and help him or her write. The most important part is to make writing a fun, exciting, and positive experience.)

Tips and Techniques

Now you have one letter on the strip. Don't panic! Getting started takes a long time in the beginning stages. Just remember to keep the sentences short. Your patience will pay off soon.

12. Repeat the word by segmenting the sounds. Help children hear the next sound. If it is a silent letter or an uncommon sound, write the letter for the class. This also speeds up the process so the focus can be on the planned learning.

13. Choose children to each write the letter that makes each sound.

14. When you come to a new word, select a child to be the spacer. This child will put two fingers or a spacing stick on the page to mark a space between the words.

15. Repeat the text just written, pointing to the word that has just been written. With the children, identify the next word, segment it, and identify the beginning sound. You might want to choose a new color marker to help the children distinguish between the words.

16. Continue this process until the sentence is completed. Remember to reread the text before adding each new word.

17. After writing the last word, ask children about ending punctuation (e.g., period, question mark, or exclamation point), and ask a child to write the ending punctuation.

18. Reread the text once more while counting the words in the sentence. Your first piece of interactive writing is now complete!

19. Display the writing in the classroom for rereading. The next day, before you begin interactive writing, reread this sentence. Then, continue with the interactive writing process.

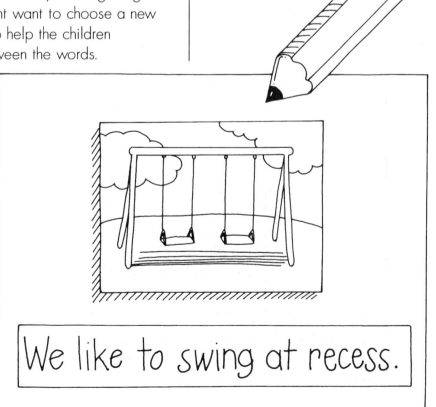

We like to swing at recess.

Quick Activity Ideas

Use the following ideas at the beginning of the year or for first attempts at interactive writing.

- Make a list of needs for the class pet. Each day, add a new need to the list during interactive writing. Put the pages together into a book in the shape of the pet.
- Make a list of favorites, such as foods, sports, or ice-cream flavors, and write repetitive, predictable sentences to record them. For example, *We like* _____.
- Trace a large paper doll for each child. Glue a sentence strip to each doll. Every day, use interactive writing to write on a doll something the child likes that begins with the same letter as his or her name. For example, *Trisha likes turtles.* Invite the child to decorate the paper doll to match the sentence.

- Brainstorm classroom rules with children, and write the rules on a chart during interactive writing. Have each child sign his or her name on the chart.
- Invite children to label the classroom with environmental print, such as *window, door,* and *sink.*
- Create a list of books the class has read or books by a favorite author.
- Brainstorm topics children want to learn about, and write the topics on a list during interactive writing. Refer back to the list throughout the year.
- Invite the class to help write the schedule for the day. Allow them to check off each task as it is completed. This helps them understand how much needs to be done before lunch, recess, or going home.
- Have children record places they have visited on vacations. For example, *Marco went to the beach. Sammy went to Hawaii.* Place the pages into a large sun-shaped book.

Morning Message

The morning message is a brief message about recent or upcoming class or school events, something a child wants to share, or information about what the class will do that day. Write a message about the day on the board when children walk into the room. Invite children to help you decide what should be included in the morning message. This is a good time to let a child of the day include a sentence about himself or herself. Have children write their names and known high-frequency words in the morning message. Ask the children to sit down and read the message together. Track the print, point out known words, or use the message to introduce or reinforce a teaching point (e.g., locate chunks of words, punctuation, parts of speech, names). Extend the morning message activity to other parts of the day. An end-of-the-day message works well in any writing mode—modeled, shared, or interactive writing. It helps tie together what the children learned and did throughout the day so when their families say *What did you do today?* their children won't say *nothing*.

Interactive Writing Extensions

After completing the interactive writing process, consider some of the following suggestions for extending children's learning and displaying their work during each stage.

All Stages

- Display past interactive writing, and have children reread it daily as part of your shared reading.
- Invite one child at a time to search for a word on a word wall that is in the interactive writing. Invite the child to circle the word with Wikki Stix. If you do not have Wikki Stix, cut a hole in an index card to make a frame, or have the children simply "frame" the word with two fingers—one finger on each side of the high-frequency word they found.

Emergent Stage

- Create rhyme riddles for the children to solve. For example, if the interactive writing says *We like to eat pizza for lunch,* you could say *I spy a word that rhymes with bike.* The children say the rhyming word *like.* Invite one child to frame the word with his or her fingers.

- Reinforce capitalization and punctuation practice. Have children point to the capital letters and punctuation.
- Have children practice sound matching and phonics skills as they relate words in the text to their names or names of pets in your classroom. For example, if the interactive writing says *The Little Red Hen did not share the bread with her friends,* you could say *I spy a word that starts with the same sound as our friend Rachel's name.* The class says *red,* and Rachel points to the word. Extend this lesson by having the class count the letters in *Rachel* and in *red.* Compare which word has more or fewer letters.
- Help children distinguish letters from words. For example, say *I spy a word with four letters.* A volunteer identifies the word or words and shows them to the rest of the class. Count the letters with the class to verify the child's answer. Use magnetic letters to make and break apart that word so children see how letters make up words.

Developing Stage

- Have children practice reading phrases smoothly. Model how to read a phrase of about three words at a time. Use your hands or construction paper strips to block off a phrase, read it, and have children repeat it. Continue the modeling with the entire text. Then, challenge children to read the text with phrasing by themselves.

- Teach and/or reinforce blends, digraphs, and endings. In the sentences *We baked some delicious chocolate chip cookies today. Then, we ate them and drank red fruit punch,* you could ask children to locate a blend, a digraph, or an ending, such as /ch/, /ed/, or /ay/.

- Have children work on linking words to their word families. Invite individual children to come up to the easel or board and locate a given word. (Choose a word that can generate word families.) Then, have children brainstorm other words that have the same rime. For example, if the story says *We baked some delicious chocolate chip cookies today. Then, we ate them and drank red fruit punch,* you could say *Who can come up and show us the word* chip? After a child comes up and frames the word with his or her fingers, say *What other words do you know that rhyme with* chip? Have children write the words on the board that have the /ip/ rime. Use a different-colored marker to highlight *ip* in each word.

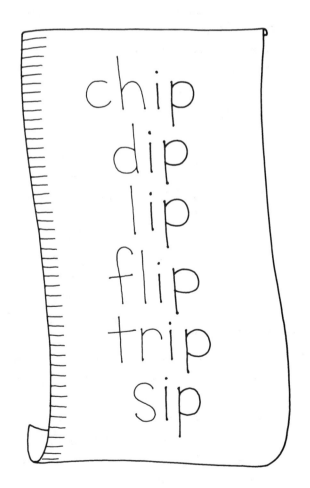

Advanced Stage

- Teach and/or reinforce how vowels change words. If the class story says *We went on a nature walk,* you could take a word such as *went* and show the class how to change the vowel to an *a* to make the word *want.*

- Teach and/or reinforce the process of revising and editing. After rereading a class story many times, ask children how they could make it even better so readers can picture it in their heads. Suggest that children add more adjectives to the story. Model how to use a caret to add an adjective. For example, a sentence from the story might say *Our tadpole turned into a frog.* Use carets to revise the sentence to say *Our tiny tadpole turned into a big, green frog.*

- Teach and/or reinforce the parts of speech (e.g., noun, verb, adjective, and pronoun). After rereading a class story many times, ask individual children to locate nouns, verbs, adjectives, and/or pronouns. Have children underline and color-code the words for further discussion. For example, have children underline nouns in red and verbs in green. For even more fun, challenge the class to find a specific noun or adjective. If text from the story says *It is raining so hard outside that we will have to eat lunch in our classroom today. Yeah!,* you could say *Who can find the verb that describes what we will be doing?* A child comes up and shows the class the word *eat.* Or, you could say *I see a noun. It is also a compound word. It has the /oo/ sound. What is the noun?* A child comes up and shows the class the word *classroom.* You will reinforce compound words, sounds, and parts of speech with this kind of riddle. Children love it!

Our ⌃tadpole
   tiny
turned into
a ⌃frog.
  ⌃
big, green

Assessment

The interactive writing process provides many opportunities to assess children. As children go up to the easel and write selected letters and/or words and word parts, watch them engage in constructing words. Note which words children know how to write quickly and easily, how they use letter-sound relationships, which spelling patterns they pay attention to, and which strategies they use to write new words. Teaching and assessment during interactive writing are linked together because the teacher is constantly determining what skills the children need to learn, practice, or review.

Use the Assessment reproducible (page 75) to assess what children are learning during interactive writing. To accurately assess each child, take time to observe individual children during each interactive writing lesson. Write the child's name on the reproducible, and mark the box next to each skill that you observe. Use a plus sign to indicate mastery, a check to indicate an adequate grasp of the concept or skill, and a minus to indicate a need for improvement or further training. The skills listed are arranged in two sections to address both emergent and more advanced stages of interactive writing. Make notes in the last section to record letters, words, and/or word chunks that the child writes easily and those with which the child needs more practice.

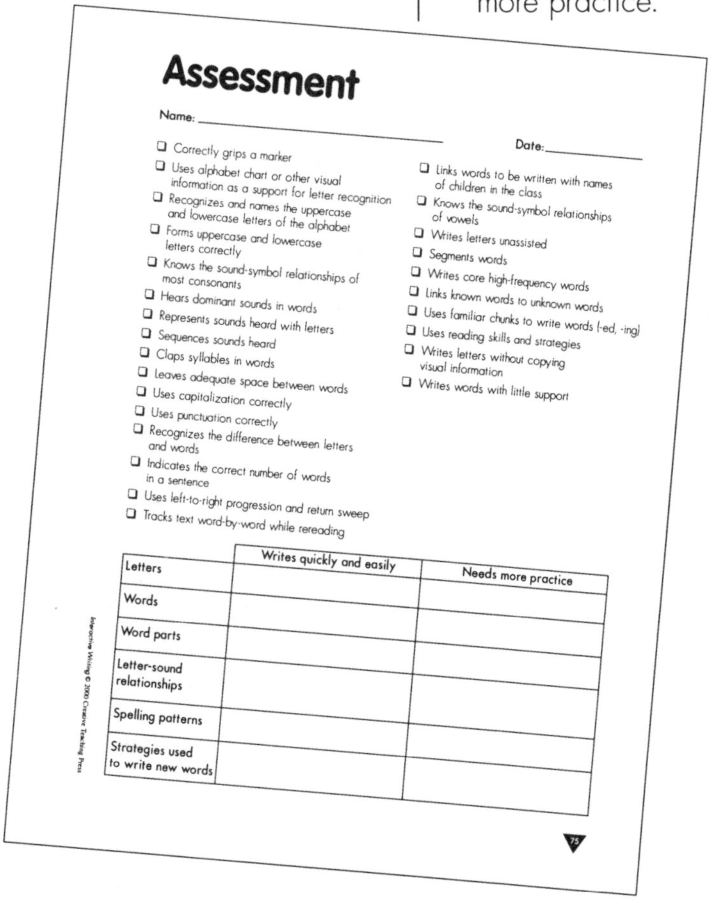

Assessment

Name: _____

Date: _____

❑ Correctly grips a marker
❑ Uses alphabet chart or other visual information as a support for letter recognition
❑ Recognizes and names the uppercase and lowercase letters of the alphabet
❑ Forms uppercase and lowercase letters correctly
❑ Knows the sound-symbol relationships of most consonants
❑ Hears dominant sounds in words
❑ Represents sounds heard with letters
❑ Sequences sounds heard
❑ Claps syllables in words
❑ Leaves adequate space between words
❑ Uses capitalization correctly
❑ Uses punctuation correctly
❑ Recognizes the difference between letters and words
❑ Indicates the correct number of words in a sentence
❑ Uses left-to-right progression and return sweep
❑ Tracks text word-by-word while rereading

❑ Links words to be written with names of children in the class
❑ Knows the sound-symbol relationships of vowels
❑ Writes letters unassisted
❑ Segments words
❑ Writes core high-frequency words
❑ Links known words to unknown words
❑ Uses familiar chunks to write words (-ed, -ing)
❑ Uses reading skills and strategies
❑ Writes letters without copying visual information
❑ Writes words with little support

	Writes quickly and easily	Needs more practice
Letters		
Words		
Word parts		
Letter-sound relationships		
Spelling patterns		
Strategies used to write new words		

Interactive Writing © 2001 Creative Teaching Press

Retell It!

Materials

- familiar storybook
- butcher paper
- scissors
- interactive writing materials

Read aloud a familiar story and discuss it with the class. As you discuss the story, guide children to identify the main events. Cut several large sheets of butcher paper into the shape of a character or an important object from the story. Each day, use interactive writing to add one important event in sequence on each page. This will help children retell and sequence events in the story. Before children write additional important events, reread with the class the previous interactive writing pages. Bind the shaped pages together into a big book, and reread it during shared reading time.

She ate the porridge.

She broke the chair.

The bears came home.

Shared Reading

Use the big book the class created (above) to teach and reinforce skills and strategies such as searching for word chunks (known parts in words), searching for known letters of the alphabet, locating punctuation or capital letters, and locating known words. Have children locate letters, word chunks, or punctuation marks and circle or underline them using Wikki Stix. Or, make word finders by cutting holes in flyswatters.

Three Main Parts

When retelling a story during later stages of interactive writing, focus children's attention on story elements such as the beginning, middle, and end of the story or the problem and solution of the story. Cut large sheets of butcher paper into the shape of a character or an important object from the story. Guide children to identify the beginning, middle, and ending story elements or identify the main problem and solution from the story, and use interactive writing to record the story elements on separate sheets of the shaped paper. This process will help children with retelling and sequencing the events. Have children reread the previous interactive writing pages before adding new pages. Bind the shaped pages together into a book, which can be reread for shared reading.

Materials

- butcher paper
- scissors
- interactive writing materials

The Cat in the Hat came to play on a rainy day.

The Cat in the Hat made a mess.

The Cat in the Hat left the house.

Shared Reading

Have children compare and contrast different versions of the same story on a Venn diagram. After the interactive writing lessons, read two versions of the same story, such as *Red Riding Hood* and *Lon Po Po* by Ed Young. Make a Venn diagram on a large piece of butcher paper using the shape of an object or a character from the story, and record children's observations of similarities and differences between the two versions.

What's Your Recipe?

Materials

- items needed for recipe
- butcher paper
- scissors
- glue
- sentence strips or cash-register tape
- interactive writing materials

Brainstorm with your class a food item that can be easily made in the classroom, such as an ice-cream sundae. Narrow the choices down to five food items, and have the class vote on a favorite food item to make. Use a simple recipe to make the food, and give each child a small serving to eat. Next, cut a large sheet of butcher paper into the shape of your food item, if possible. Glue on sentence strips or cash-register tape or draw lines on the butcher paper. Recall with the class what was needed to make the recipe. Through the interactive writing process, list the ingredients and the steps for making the food item. At the beginning stages, you may want to limit each page to one sentence. Children at the later stages can list the ingredients on one page and the steps on another.

Shared Reading

Write a "mystery" recipe on the board by listing the ingredients and the steps for making that food without naming what it makes. Use shared reading to have children read the recipe and discover what it is a recipe for. Then, invite children to make the recipe at a center and serve some for all to enjoy!

Let's Make a Mask!

Invite each child to design a mask from a paper plate and glue a paint stick or strip of folded tagboard to the back for a handle. After children make their mask, have them practice oral language and sequencing skills. Ask each child to describe the steps he or she took in making a mask. Tell the class that you want to make your own mask and you need them to help you with the materials list and the steps. Use the interactive writing process to list their suggestions on butcher paper. Once the steps have been sequenced, read them with the class while you make the mask. You may want to invite a principal or parent volunteer to read the steps and make a mask, too.

Materials

- paper plates
- art supplies (e.g., construction paper, scissors, glue, sequins, glitter, feathers, yarn)
- paint sticks or tagboard
- butcher paper
- interactive writing materials

How to Make a Mask

1. Get a paper plate.
2. Draw your mask design.
3. Cut out eye holes.
4. Glue on feathers and sequins to make a face.

Shared Reading

Type the sequenced steps from the interactive writing process. Send home with each child a few art supplies and a copy of the steps attached to a paper plate. Invite children to read the steps while a family member creates a mask. Ask children to bring the mask back to share with the class.

The Three Bears' House

Materials

- *Goldilocks and the Three Bears* (any version)
- Sequencing Cards (page 76)
- crayons or markers
- scissors
- pocket chart
- butcher paper
- tempera paint/paintbrushes
- sentence strips or cash-register tape
- glue
- interactive writing materials

Shared Reading

Enlarge the Porridge Recipe reproducible (page 77) for Three Bears' Porridge. Read aloud *Goldilocks and the Three Bears*. Read the recipe with the class, and fill in the blanks with the ingredients that the class decides upon. Invite children to make and eat the porridge.

Read aloud any version of *Goldilocks and the Three Bears* a few times, and then discuss the main events in order. Color and cut out the Sequencing Cards. Have the class sequence the cards in order in a pocket chart. Discuss the events of the story. Label the cards with numbers to show which event occurred first, second, and so on. Next, have children create a story map. Divide the class into three groups, and give each group a large butcher paper rectangle. Have each group paint a different room from the Three Bears' house. Ask children what event happened first in the story. Using the interactive writing process, have children write on sentence strips or cash-register tape about what happened first. Glue this text to the correct room of the house. You can add one event each session, depending on your class and their attention span. Continue until you have completed the story map. Read the new story together. For example, *First, Goldilocks went into their home. She ate the porridge. Baby Bear's was just right. She sat in the chairs. Baby Bear's broke. She went upstairs. She got in Baby Bear's bed and fell asleep. The Three Bears came home. She went out the window and ran away.*

Grandma's House

Read aloud any version of *Little Red Riding Hood,* and discuss the sequence of events. Use a graphic organizer to record children's ideas on the chalkboard. Have children paint a forest scene with a path on butcher paper, and then add three-dimensional artwork, such as twisted butcher paper trees, tissue paper flowers, and a pretzel stick roof for Grandmother's house. Have each child cut out the Wolf and Little Red Riding Hood pictures from the reproducible, color them, and glue them to craft sticks to make interactive characters for acting out the story. Staple an envelope to the story map to store one set of the characters. Use the interactive writing process to have children write about the events in order. Have them write one event each day that explains the main idea of that section of the story. For example, *Little Red Riding Hood went to visit her grandmother. She was bringing her some lunch. The wolf was following her.* Glue the writing onto the story map in sequence along the path in the forest.

Materials

- *Little Red Riding Hood* (any version)
- butcher paper (assorted colors)
- tempera paint/paintbrushes
- tissue paper (assorted colors)
- pretzel sticks
- scissors
- Wolf and Little Red Riding Hood reproducible (page 78)
- crayons or markers
- craft sticks
- glue
- stapler
- envelope
- interactive writing materials

Independent Writing

After reading aloud other versions of *Little Red Riding Hood,* invite each child to create his or her own version. Model how children could change the characters, setting, or ending to create their story. Type the children's stories and put them in a class book for shared reading. Ask each child to read his or her story to the class for oral language practice.

What Do You See?

Materials

- *Brown Bear, Brown Bear* by Bill Martin, Jr.
- butcher paper
- tempera paint/paintbrushes
- scissors
- stapler
- paper towels
- cash-register tape (optional)
- speech bubbles
- special reading pointer
- special reading glasses
- interactive writing materials

This activity works very well with the old favorite *Brown Bear, Brown Bear*, but any book can be used. After reading aloud the story several times, divide the class into pairs, help each pair sketch the outline of an animal from the story on a large sheet of butcher paper, and have children paint their animal. When the paint is dry, place each paper on another piece of butcher paper, and cut out an additional animal shape. Have children staple the edges of their two pieces together, leaving one small section open. Have students stuff the inside with paper towels, and staple the last section closed. Display the three-dimensional animals on a bulletin board. Beginning with Brown Bear, ask children what animal he sees next to him on the bulletin board. Draw lines on or glue cash-register tape to a speech bubble for children to write on. Use interactive writing to have children write in the speech bubble *I see a _____ _____ looking at me*. Post the speech bubble with the appropriate animal. Continue with one new animal each day. Before adding each new speech bubble, reread the previous speech bubbles with the class. Use a special reading pointer, such as a large painted dowel dipped in glitter or a flyswatter with a center hole cut out, to point to each word. Invite children to wear "special reading glasses"—sunglasses with the lenses popped out and ribbons tied to the frames— while reading aloud.

Language Experience

Have children act out the story, sequencing their painted animals before displaying the animals on the bulletin board. Invite children to tell you about their experience, and record it on speech bubbles. Display the dictation on the bulletin board next to the animals.

Photo Fun

Display in a pocket chart photos from a field trip or class activity. Include many children in the same photo, but make sure each child is in at least one photograph. Display a speech bubble on an easel. Choose a picture from the pocket chart, and ask the children featured in the picture what the speech bubble should say. Then, have the children in the photo come up and use interactive writing to write in the speech bubble. For example, next to a picture of children milking a cow, children could write *We got to milk the big, brown jersey cow. Her name was Elsie.* When children have interactively written about each photo, glue each photo and its speech bubble onto a sheet of construction paper. Bind these pages into a class book for rereading.

Materials

- photos from a field trip or class activity
- pocket chart
- speech bubbles
- glue
- construction paper
- bookbinding materials
- interactive writing materials

Independent Reading

Let each child write a statement in a speech bubble about his or her favorite part of the field trip or activity. Bind these papers into another class book. When making class books, always include a table of contents. Children quickly learn to use it if their name is included! Also, include a reader response page (i.e., a page for readers to write about thoughts they had about the book) at the end of all class books. Children love reading what parents and class visitors have written about their writing. Send home this book and the photo fun class book in a special backpack with related literature to be shared with children's families.

Add the Words

Materials

- wordless storybook (2 copies)
- scissors or paper cutter
- glue
- construction paper
- sentence strips or cash-register tape
- bookbinding materials
- interactive writing materials

A story innovation is when children rewrite, change the ending, or change one element of a story using their own words. Wordless books are ideal for interactive writing since their illustrations stimulate creative thinking. Show the wordless storybook to the class, and discuss with children what happens in the story. Then, cut out the illustrations from the two books. (Two copies are necessary because illustrations may be back to back.) Glue each illustration onto a separate sheet of construction paper, and number the pages. Glue sentence strips or cash-register tape to the bottom of each page. Use the interactive writing process to write about a new page every day. Before beginning each new page, have children reread the previous pages to make sure the new page flows with the story. Bind the finished book pages, and put the book in your book corner. Use this story for shared reading activities.

The boy and the snowman flew through the air.

6

Independent Reading

Place class photos in a photo album. Place an index card in the slot following each photo. Invite children to look through the album, choose a picture, and write about it on the index card next to it. Have children return their index card to the album so others can read the captions.

Alphabet Books

Read a variety of alphabet books with the class. Discuss the similarities of the books. Tell the class that they will make a giant alphabet book about something related to a theme or topic they are learning about. For example, they might make an alphabet book about friends, animals, or the zoo. Place magnetic letters in a paper sack. Ask each child to pull a letter out of the sack. Have children close their eyes and use their sense of touch to identify the letter they selected. Ask each child to draw a picture on white paper of something related to the theme that starts with that letter. If children have trouble thinking of an item that starts with their letter, invite them to look through alphabet books. Invite children to share their finished picture. Glue each picture to a separate sheet of construction or butcher paper. Glue a die-cut letter to the top of each sheet. At the beginning stages, use the interactive writing process to create a one-word label for each picture. At later stages, have children write a sentence such as _____ *starts with the letter* _____ for each page. Bind the sheets together to make a class alphabet book.

Materials

- alphabet books
- magnetic letters
- paper sack
- white drawing paper
- markers, watercolors, or crayons
- glue
- construction or butcher paper
- die-cut letters
- bookbinding materials
- interactive writing materials

Independent Reading

Create a take-home bag that includes magnetic letters, the class-made alphabet book, a cookie sheet, a resealable plastic bag of children's photos, and the Alphabet Bag Note reproducible (page 79). Each night, invite a child to take home the sack and follow the instructions on the reproducible. Be sure to add your own photo to the book and sign your name.

Who Will Help?

Materials

- *The Little Red Hen* (several versions)
- crayons or markers
- children's photos
- glue
- construction paper
- bookbinding materials
- interactive writing materials

Read aloud several versions of *The Little Red Hen*. Then, brainstorm with children new characters (perhaps the children themselves), a new setting, a new food to make, and a new ending. Instead of making bread, the main character could make chocolate chip cookies or some other tasty treat. Through shared writing, list the basic ingredients and student-generated steps to make the food in your story. For example, for chocolate chip cookies, you could record *Ingredients: sugar, flour, butter, eggs, and chocolate chips.* Use the interactive writing process to list who will help make the food item. You will be the main character. For example, on day one, your class might write *"Who will help me add the sugar?" "Not us,"* said Chloe, Miguel, and Sonya. "We want to paint." "Then I will do it myself," said Mrs. Lee. Continue this text format using all the children. Use this opportunity to teach how to write dialogue and use quotation marks. Have the class write the ending after discussing it. Ask children to add illustrations to the finished story. You could also include children's photos. Glue the text with illustrations and/or photos onto sheets of construction paper, and bind the pages into a class book.

Shared Reading

Write the recipe for making a food item on chart paper. Follow the recipe and make the treat with the class. Yum! Give each child a copy of the recipe to take home.

Through My Eyes

Read aloud any version of the *Three Little Pigs* that depicts the wolf as a "bad" character. Discuss the story and how each pig feels about what happened. Tell the class that this story is told from the pigs' point of view. Ask them how the wolf's version of the same story would differ from the other characters' versions. Tell children that they are going to pretend they are the wolf. Remind them about wolf facts, such as wolves hunt for food and eat meat. Have the class brainstorm a new version of the story told by the wolf. Use the interactive writing process to write the children's story on chart paper. For example, the first part of the story might begin with *I was very hungry, and I wanted to make a pizza. I went next door to borrow some cheese from Little Pig. He was so rude! He slammed the door in my face, and it made me sneeze. I didn't mean to blow over his house.* Save room at the bottom of each page for a large picture. Invite children to work with partners to illustrate the story. Then, read aloud *The True Story of the Three Little Pigs,* and discuss how this version compared to the children's version.

Materials

- *Three Little Pigs*
- chart paper
- crayons or markers
- *The True Story of the Three Little Pigs* by John Scieszka
- interactive writing materials

Shared Reading

Type the completed story, and create a mini-book for each child to illustrate. Have children take home their book to read to their family.

Penguin Facts

Materials

- Tacky the Penguin books by Helen Lester
- nonfiction books about penguins
- 6' (1.8 m) sheet of black butcher paper
- scissors
- construction paper (assorted colors)
- sentence strips
- glue
- fishing wire
- dowel
- ribbons
- glitter
- paper or plastic fish
- interactive writing materials

Read aloud several Tacky the Penguin books and nonfiction books about penguins in preparation for the activity. Draw and cut out a huge penguin on black butcher paper. Have children help you decorate both sides of the penguin. Make one side look like Tacky wearing his funny clothes and the other side look like a real penguin. Use the interactive writing process to write facts about Tacky on sentence strips, and glue the strips to the Tacky side of the penguin. Then, have children write facts about real penguins, and glue the sentence strips to the other side of the penguin. Use fishing wire to display the penguin from the ceiling so both sides can be seen. Decorate a dowel with ribbons and glitter. Glue a paper or plastic fish to one end. Invite children to use the dowel as a reading pointer when rereading the fiction and nonfiction facts about penguins.

Independent Writing

Have each child complete the sentence frames on the Penguin reproducible (page 80) to compare Tacky with real penguins. Invite children to share their completed frames with the class.

Turtle Truths

Read aloud several Franklin books and nonfiction books about turtles. Draw a huge turtle on green butcher paper, and cut it out. Label one side *Franklin* and the other side *Real Turtles*. Use the interactive writing process to write facts about Franklin on sentence strips, and glue the strips to the Franklin side of the turtle. Then, have children write facts about real turtles, and glue the strips to the other side of the turtle. Use fishing wire to display the turtle from the ceiling so both sides can be seen.

Materials

- Franklin books by Paulette Bourgeois
- nonfiction books about turtles
- 6' (1.8 m) sheet of green butcher paper
- scissors
- sentence strips
- glue
- fishing wire
- interactive writing materials

Franklin
goes to school
likes to play
is scared of the dark
has a pet goldfish

Real Turtles
live a long time
Sleep in their shells
crawl slowly

Independent Writing

Give each child a Turtle reproducible (page 81). Have children compare and contrast Franklin with real turtles based on the books you shared. Invite children to list their observations about real turtles and characteristics of Franklin on the reproducible.

Elmer the Elephant

Materials

- Elmer books by David McKee
- Elephant reproducible (page 82)
- dot paints or tempera paint/paintbrushes
- glue
- construction paper
- bookbinding materials
- interactive writing materials

An author study gives children the opportunity to learn about an author's writing style. Focus on comparing different stories, repeating characters, or plot changes. This author study will focus on David McKee's character, Elmer. After reading aloud several stories about Elmer, brainstorm facts about him with the class. For example, you could write the sentence frame *Elmer likes to _____* or *Elmer can _____*. Each day, use interactive writing to write facts about Elmer. When you have enough facts to create a book, have children work in pairs to paint a copy of the Elephant reproducible in a patchwork design and complete the sentence frame. Have students cut out their elephant and glue it and the interactive writing to construction paper. Bind these pages into a class book.

Elmer likes to play hide-and-seek.

Shared Reading

Draw a giant elephant on butcher paper, and cut it out to create a word bank. If you make it one-sided, include words related to the author study and elephant facts. If you make it two-sided, write fact words on one side and words related to Elmer on the other. Then, use fishing wire to display the elephant from the ceiling.

Nice Mice Lessons

Cut several pieces of construction paper into large mouse shapes. Over the course of a week, share with children at least five of Leo Lionni's books that involve mice as characters. Each day, read a new book, and discuss why the author wrote the book and what lesson he wants the reader to learn. Then, use the interactive writing process to write this message on sentence strips and glue the strips to the construction paper mice. When you have finished reading the books and writing about the lessons, bind the mice into a class book titled *Leo Lionni's Lessons*. You can now have children study the author while rereading the class book.

Materials

- construction paper
- scissors
- mouse books by Leo Lionni
- sentence strips
- glue
- interactive writing materials

Mice Lessons

We should share poetry with others. It's important to be ourselves. Be a good friend.

Independent Writing

Invite children to help create a giant mobile. Draw a giant mouse and pieces of cheese on butcher paper, and cut them out. Trace the mouse shape on another sheet of butcher paper, and cut it out. Staple the edges of the mouse shapes together, leaving one small section open. Stuff the inside with paper towels or newspaper, and staple the last section closed. Have each child write on the cheese a positive character trait, such as *Be honest, Share, Be kind,* or *Say nice things.* Use fishing line to attach the cheese to the mouse, and display it for rereading.

Write Back Soon!

Materials

- chart paper
- stamps or stickers
- envelope
- writing paper
- interactive writing materials

Draw lines on a large sheet of chart paper. Discuss with children the five parts of a letter—heading, greeting, body, closing, and signature. Write a letter to other classrooms, community helpers, school personnel, or authors. Begin the interactive writing process to write the letter. For children in the emergent stages of writing, you might have children only write one part (e.g., heading or greeting) of the letter each day. Children at the later stages can write the entire letter in one session. When the letter is finished, invite children to decorate it with a border of stamps or stickers. During another lesson, have children address an envelope for sending the letter. When they finish, let the children deliver the note along with some paper for the person to write a note back to your class.

Independent Writing

As a homework assignment, have children bring to school a stamped envelope addressed to a relative or friend. Have children copy the school address for the return address. Have each child write a letter on the Letter reproducible (page 83) and mail it. The entire class will enjoy writing letters and receiving responses. Post the responses for all to read. For added fun, find another class who would like to exchange letters with your class.

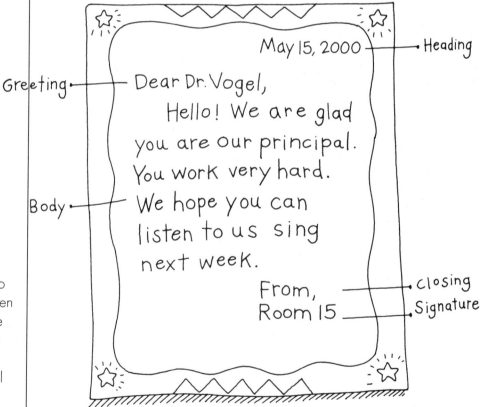

Heading — May 15, 2000

Greeting — Dear Dr. Vogel,

Body — Hello! We are glad you are our principal. You work very hard. We hope you can listen to us sing next week.

Closing — From,

Signature — Room 15

Gratefully Yours

Brainstorm with children names of people at the school whom they would like to thank. It could be cafeteria help, the principal, the custodian, or another teacher or class. Discuss the importance of acknowledging acts of kindness. Use scalloped-edged scissors to cut a large sheet of butcher paper into a heart shape. Draw lines on the butcher paper, or glue sentence strips or cash-register tape to it. Use the interactive writing process to write the thank-you note. Let children deliver the finished note.

Materials
- butcher paper
- scalloped-edged scissors
- sentence strips or cash-register tape
- glue
- interactive writing materials

Dear Ms. Cochran,
Thank you for reading us a story. It was a funny book.
Love,
Room 12

Independent Writing
Now that you have taught the class the importance of writing thank-you notes, have each child write a note to a friend or family member on stationery.

Humpty Dumpty

Materials

- 3' x 2' (1 m x 61 cm) sheets of white butcher paper
- scissors
- sponges
- pastel-colored paints
- paintbrushes
- construction paper
- glue
- sentence strips
- bookbinding materials
- interactive writing materials

Cut butcher paper into large egg shapes, enough for each pair of children to have one. Invite pairs to sponge-paint their egg in pastel colors. Have children paint a bow tie and a face and cut a hat, arms, and legs from construction paper to make Humpty Dumpty. Each day, select one Humpty Dumpty, and brainstorm with the class a simple rhyme for it, such as *Humpty Dumpty sat on a <u>tree</u>. Humpty Dumpty fell on a <u>bee</u>.* Use interactive writing to record the rhyme on sentence strips. When each Humpty Dumpty egg has a rhyme, bind the eggs together into a class book for rereading.

Shared Writing

Have children brainstorm new altered rhymes for other nursery rhymes. Write a sentence frame from a nursery rhyme, and ask the class to create a new rhyme for it. For example, *There was an old woman who lived in a <u>hat</u>. She <u>had a lot of dogs, but loved her cat</u>; Little Miss <u>Anna</u> sat on a <u>banana</u>;* or *Hickory, Dickory <u>Dare</u>, the mouse ran up the <u>chair</u>.* Invite children to work with a partner and choose one rhyme to illustrate. Bind the poems into a class rhyming book.

Rhyming Detectives

Recite several nursery rhymes with children to prepare them to become "Rhyming Detectives." Discuss with children the main ideas of favorite nursery rhymes. Use the format of questioning that includes asking *who, what, when, where, how,* and *why* to form questions about a nursery rhyme whose answer rhymes with the question. For example, *Who sat on a tuffet? Little Miss Muffet. What was lost by Little Bo Peep? Her sheep.* Use the interactive writing process to record several detective questions and answers on sentence strips or cash-register tape, and glue each question to the outside of a folded piece of construction paper. Glue the answer to each question on the inside of the paper. Have children paint nursery rhyme scenes and characters on a large sheet of butcher paper and glue the questions next to the corresponding character. Post the butcher paper on a wall, and have children come up to a question, solve it, and lift the flap to check their answer.

Materials

- nursery rhymes
- construction paper
- tempera paints/paintbrushes
- butcher paper
- glue
- interactive writing materials

Shared Reading and Writing

Create new versions of nursery rhymes using classmates' names. For example, *Hickory, Dickory, Dock. Luca ran up the clock. The clock struck two. Away she flew. Hickory, Dickory, Dock!* Reread these for shared reading.

Diamond Poems

Materials

- poetry
- chart paper
- Poetry Pocket reproducible (page 84)
- crayons or markers
- scissors
- glue
- construction paper
- stapler
- interactive writing materials

Read aloud different forms of poetry. Tell children that they will be writing some of their own poetry. Ask the class to choose an object related to a theme you are studying. Use interactive writing to write the name of that object on chart paper inside a diamond shape. Have the class choose two words to describe the object and record those words below the first words. Ask children to name three words that tell what the object does and record them below the last words. Have children think of another word for the object and write that at the bottom of the diamond shape. This poem provides a great opportunity to teach and/or reinforce the parts of speech. Try to create at least three different poems so children feel confident with the format. You may wish to type the finished poems so children can illustrate and share them with their families. Have each child color a Poetry Pocket reproducible, cut it out, and glue it to a sheet of construction paper folded in the shape of a pocket and stapled on three sides. Give children a copy of the completed poems to put in their Poetry Pocket.

Independent Writing

Have children use the Diamond Poem reproducible (page 85) to create their own poems. Have children write the name of an object on the first line and working from top to bottom, have them fill in a single word in each remaining blank. Tell children not to try to have their poem make sense, but to let their imagination lead the poem wherever it wants to go.

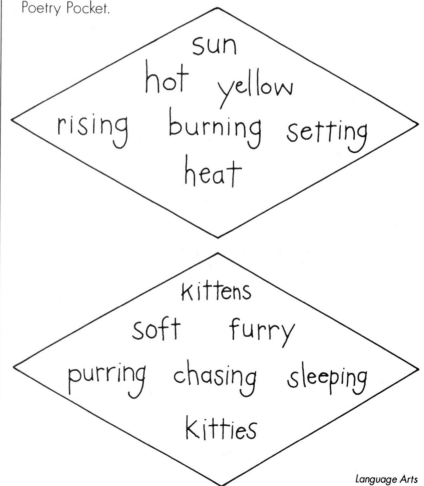

Limericks

Read aloud different limericks so children get a feel for how limericks sound. A limerick is a humorous, playful rhyme that has five lines. The first, second, and fifth lines rhyme. The third and fourth lines rhyme, but are slightly shorter. Select a topic for a limerick from current units your class is studying. Brainstorm ideas about your topic with the class. For example, during a pet theme, have children brainstorm all the things one pet likes to do. Then, have children suggest rhyming words that relate to the pet, and record their responses on chart paper. Depending on the children's ability level, use the interactive writing process to write one line of the limerick, each day or the entire limerick at once. Type the finished limerick, and give each child a copy to illustrate and share with his or her family. Have children include a copy of the completed limerick in their Poetry Pocket.

Materials

- limericks
- chart paper
- crayons or markers
- interactive writing materials
- Poetry Pocket reproducible (page 84)

There was a small puppy named Spot.
He played and swam a lot.
He went in the pool
Because it felt cool.
The summers are always so hot.

Keep a poem in your pocket!

Mitch's

Poetry Pocket

Shared Writing

Each week create a simple limerick with the class about the special person of the week. Include favorite activities, favorite foods, or other special things about the child. Trace the child's body on butcher paper, and record the limerick in the middle.

Sophie likes to play soccer.
She keeps her shoes in her locker.
She runs very fast.
No one can get past.
That's why she's so good at soccer.

Community Places

Materials

- camera/film
- die-cut letters
- glue
- construction paper
- sentence strips or cash-register tape
- tape
- interactive writing materials

A fun way to use interactive writing while learning about the community is to use photos of familiar places, such as local restaurants, fast-food restaurants, stores, and theaters. Take one photo of a place in your community to correspond with each letter of the alphabet. Some letters are tricky—be creative. For example, you could use ending letters for the letter x. Taking the photos is a great parent volunteer project. After developing photos of familiar places, glue each die-cut letter and a corresponding photo to the top of a sheet of construction paper. Laminate the sheets. Introduce one photo at a time, asking children what they do at the place in the photo. Use the interactive writing process to write on a sentence strip or cash-register tape about each location. Tape the writing below the photo. Reread the previous pages before introducing each new location. Keep the pages in a place where children can reread them throughout the day.

Shared Writing

Take the class on a walking field trip to one of the locations they wrote about. Many fast-food restaurants will give tours and discounts. Take photos of the location, the staff, and the children in your class. After the trip, discuss what children saw and did and write about it together. Glue photos from the field trip next to the text to enhance the story.

Social Studies

Our World

This is a great activity for beginning the school year to show children where items are located in the classroom and get them reading common words. When children write the labels themselves, they get a sense of ownership in the classroom. They also tend to notice and read the labels more often. Take children on a tour of the classroom, and then ask them what items they would like to label. Explain to them that reading the labels will·help them read and remember where things are stored. Cut white construction paper or sentence strips to use for labels, making sure they are large enough for children to read them. Use the interactive writing process to create labels for things around the room, such as *glue, crayons, bathroom, pencils, blocks, door, window, clock,* and *post office.* Also consider gluing photos, drawings, or pictures from catalogs to the writing. Display the labels next to the items in your classroom.

Materials

- white construction paper or sentence strips
- scissors
- glue
- photos, drawings, or old catalogs
- interactive writing materials

Independent Writing

Invite children to cut out pictures from magazines or catalogs and glue them to construction paper. Have children write labels for the items or cut out words from the magazines or catalogs and glue them next to the pictures. Keep the labeled collages at a center for independent reading.

I'm Special!

Materials

- large paper dolls
- scissors
- tempera paint/paintbrushes
- sentence strips or cash-register tape
- glue
- interactive writing materials

Trace a class set of large paper dolls. Select one child each week to be the "Special Person of the Week." On Monday, have the special child cut out and paint one side of a paper doll. Later that day, ask the special child one of the following questions:

- *What is your favorite color?*
- *What is your favorite food?*
- *What do you want to be when you grow up?*
- *What is your favorite book?*
- *What do you like to do in your free time?*

Use the interactive writing process to write the child's response to the question on a sentence strip or cash-register tape. Invite the child to glue the writing to the paper doll. Ask the child a different question each day. Write each sentence in a different-colored marker to help children distinguish between the sentences. At the end of the week, reread the paper doll and send it home with the child to share with his or her family.

Independent Writing

Have each child write a letter to the Special Person of the Week. Have children illustrate their letter, and then bind the letters into a book with a construction paper heart cover in the special child's favorite color. Send the book home with the child at the end of the week.

Social Studies

Worldwide Friends

During a unit on places around the world, use the interactive writing process to record information learned throughout the unit. This activity could also focus on countries or continents. Depending on the length of your unit, introduce a new country every other day or once a week. Choose one of the following sentences on which to base the interactive writing:

In _____, people like to _____.
Children in _____ like to _____.
Families in _____ like to eat _____.
In _____, people celebrate _____.
If I could fly to _____, I could see _____.
Children in _____ and the United States are the same, because

_____.

Display a world map on a bulletin board. Place photos of the children in your class around the edges of the map, and use yarn or ribbon to connect each photo to the country the child's ancestors are from. Next, display the interactive writing around the map near the country discussed. Use an additional piece of yarn or ribbon to connect each piece of writing to a country or a photo.

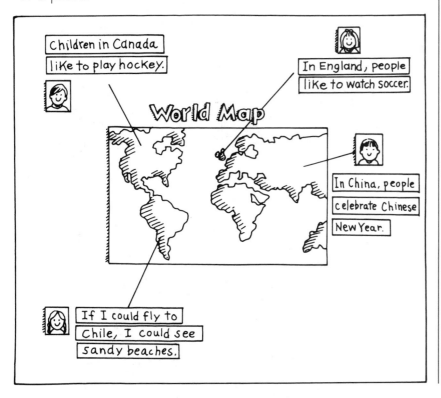

Materials

- world map
- children's photos
- yarn or ribbon
- interactive writing materials

Independent Writing

Invite each child to complete the Passport reproducible (page 86). Fold the pages, and glue a child's photo to the box. Now children are ready to travel!

Friends Photo Book

Materials

- white construction paper
- scissors
- photo album
- children's photos
- interactive writing materials

Cut several sheets of white construction paper to fit in a photo album. Draw lines on the construction paper so children can write directly on the paper. Select photos from a classroom activity or special event, such as Special Person's Day, Author's Day, or a holiday. Make a collage of the photos on one page of the photo album. Display the collage, and discuss as a class what the children see in the collage. Use the interactive writing process to describe the photos on the construction paper. When finished, return the pages to the album so the collage will be on the left side and the writing will be on the right. Continue with a few more collage pages of special events. Invite children to reread these pages often.

Independent Writing

Fill the remainder of the photo album with photos taken during various events in your classroom. Be sure that every child is in the photo book. Put a piece of lined, white construction paper on the pages opposite the pictures for writing. Attach the Parent Letter reproducible (page 87) to the cover of the photo album. Each day, invite a different child to take home the photo album. Have the child choose a photo and write a caption or story at home to go with that photo. The next day, have the child sit in the Author's Chair and read the writing to the class.

Social Studies

Long Ago Wall Story

Read aloud *Long Ago and Today* and *100 Years Ago*. Discuss with children how life has changed. Brainstorm with children categories to compare long ago with today, such as transportation, school, food, shopping, or clothing. List items that fall into each category. Fold brown butcher paper in half horizontally, draw the shape of a log cabin on it, and cut it out so you have a cabin shape on each side of the fold. Make several of these cabins from butcher paper. Invite each child to paint on construction paper an object from one of the categories discussed. Have children cut out the items and glue them onto opposite sides of the cabin so that items from long ago are on one side and items from today are on the other. Use the interactive writing process to label the items for one category each day and/or complete the frame *Long ago _____.* *Today _____.* For example, *Long ago <u>they grew their own food</u>. Today <u>we buy food</u>.* The story also serves as a word bank for further writing on the topic. Hang the wall story across the room from fishing wire so the class can see both sides of the story.

Materials

- *Long Ago and Today* by Rozanne Lanczak Williams (Creative Teaching Press)
- *100 Years Ago* by Donna Marriott (Creative Teaching Press)
- brown butcher paper
- scissors
- tempera paint/paintbrushes
- glue
- fishing wire
- interactive writing materials

Independent Writing

Share Tomie De Paola's wordless book *Pancakes for Breakfast.* Then, invite the class to make pancakes. Have each child record the recipe on the Pancake reproducible (page 88). Invite the class to make their own butter, just like people long ago. Pour a little bit of whipping cream in empty baby-food jars, and then have children shake the jars until the cream turns into butter. Add honey to make honey butter.

Social Studies

In the Jungle

Materials

- nonfiction books about the rain forest or jungle
- butcher paper
- scissors
- construction paper scraps
- tempera paint/paintbrushes
- sponges
- glue
- sentence strips or cash-register tape
- interactive writing materials

Throughout a particular unit, use the interactive writing process to record facts learned. Read aloud information from nonfiction books about animals from the rain forest or jungle. Draw the shapes of the animals on large butcher paper, and cut them out. Invite the class to help decorate the animals with construction paper scraps and paint. For example, have children sponge-paint construction paper, and after it dries, tear it into small squares to glue on a gorilla or sloth for texture. Or, have children place their hand on a sponge dipped in orange or brown paint and make handprint "spots" on a giraffe. Then, use the interactive writing process to write interesting or important facts about each animal on sentence strips or cash-register tape, such as *Sloths sleep in the canopy. They are the slowest mammal. Their hair grows upside down.* Glue the strips to the animals. Display the animals, and reread them daily. Ask questions about what was written to assess comprehension of the topic. If you do not have space in your room to display the work, compile important ideas the class has written into a book called *Five Facts about the Rain Forest* or *Five Facts about the Jungle*. Have children illustrate each fact. When you teach other science units, have the class create more fact books using the interactive writing process.

Shared Writing

Gather the following four foods that come from the rain forest: chocolate chips, banana chips, pineapple chunks, and coconut. Give children an opportunity to taste the foods. Graph their favorite rain forest foods on a banana-shaped graph, and record what children observe about the graph on a speech bubble.

Gorillas are the strongest monkey. The babies walk in a conga line. They eat plants all day.

Giraffes

Science Subjects

Select an old calendar with pictures that will generate discussion of a topic of study, such as plants, animals, or habitats. Cut the calendar apart and glue each picture onto a large piece of construction paper. Laminate the sheets so you can reuse them. Ask children to describe each picture, and use the interactive writing process to record children's responses. Display these sheets on a bulletin board, or bind them in a class book for rereading.

Materials

- old calendar
- scissors
- glue
- construction paper
- interactive writing materials

Polar bears look playful. They are the largest land meat eaters.

Independent Writing

Collect old calendars, and place them in a writing center for independent writing opportunities. Laminate the calendar pictures, and store them in a magazine holder. When children come to the center, have them choose a picture that interests them and write a caption or poem to go with it. Invite children to share their writing with the class.

Taking Care of the Earth

Materials

- tempera paints/paintbrushes
- large paper plates
- construction paper (assorted colors)
- scissors
- glue
- fishing wire (optional)
- interactive writing materials

Have children work in pairs, and invite each pair to paint a face on a large paper plate. Invite children to add construction paper eyes, nose, and hair. Have each child trace one hand on a piece of skin-tone construction paper, and cut it out. Have children glue their painted plate to the top edge of a horizontal sheet of construction paper and glue the hands to the sides of the paper. Each day, choose a paper-plate face to write a message on. Discuss what the class would like to teach others about taking care of the Earth. Use the interactive writing process to write the sentence on the construction paper. Display the signs on a wall, or attach them back to back, and hang them from the ceiling with fishing wire.

Shared Writing

Write a letter with the class to an environmental group. Ask children to describe what they have learned and how they plan to do their part in helping the Earth. Ask children to draw illustrations to mail with the group letter.

Comparing Caterpillars

Cut white butcher paper into the shape of a large silkworm. Cut green butcher paper into the shape of a large caterpillar. Use these shapes as comparison charts. Read aloud several books about silkworms and caterpillars. Set up a science investigation table with books and live silkworms and caterpillars. Include magnifying lenses for close investigation. Use the interactive writing process to have children brainstorm and write facts about what they learned and observed about the bugs. As the bugs' life cycle continues, continue to add to the comparison chart. Display these charts in the science center for rereading and as a reference for independent writing.

Materials

- white and green butcher paper
- scissors
- books about silkworms and caterpillars
- silkworms
- caterpillars
- magnifying lenses
- interactive writing materials

Silkworms make their cocoon from silk.
Silkworms become moths.

Caterpillars form a chrysalis.
Caterpillars eat lots of plants.
Some caterpillars are hairy.
Caterpillars become butterflies or moths.

Shared Writing

After reading aloud a few fictional stories about silkworms or caterpillars, have the class create a fictional story about the friendship of a silkworm and a caterpillar. Use shared writing to record the story on chart paper. Then, have each child illustrate a picture from the story on a large index card. Glue or tape these cards around the edges of the chart story to create a border. Make moth and butterfly reading sticks by placing stickers on or gluing children's drawings to the pointed end of chopsticks for children to use while rereading.

Blooming Sunflowers

Materials

- green, black, and yellow butcher paper
- stapler
- sunflower seeds
- glue
- scissors
- *The Tiny Seed* by Eric Carle
- potting soil
- paper cups
- marker
- interactive writing materials

Shared Writing

Have the class create a sunflower rhyme together, such as *My tiny seed grew and grew. Here's a sunflower just for you!* Have children copy the rhyme on the center of the Sunflower reproducible (page 89). Have each child twist tissue paper squares around the eraser end of a pencil and glue them to their sunflower. Invite children to cut out their sunflower and glue it onto a wooden skewer. Have children place their skewer in the soil with their sunflower plants and take them home.

Twist green butcher paper to make a giant stem, and staple it to a bulletin board. Add huge green butcher paper leaves. Glue sunflower seeds to a large black paper circle to make the center of a sunflower and staple the circle to the stem. Cut out several giant yellow petals from butcher paper. Draw writing lines on the petals. Read aloud *The Tiny Seed*, and then help children plant their own sunflower seeds in paper cups. (It is best to plant at least 3—4 seeds in each cup.) Have children check the seed cups every few days. When any changes occur, use the interactive writing process to have children record them on the petals. (Be sure children use pencil so errors can be erased. White magic fix-it tape will not have the same effect on the yellow paper.) Then, trace over the writing with a marker to reread. After each writing session, add the petal to the bulletin board. Continue until children's sunflowers bloom.

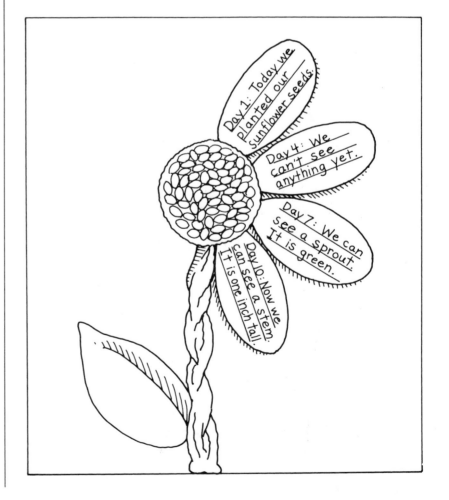

Science

Hatch a Chick

Set up a chick "investigation center" to monitor the development of baby chicks. Read aloud nonfiction books about chicks that give facts and show pictures of each stage of development. Cut out a giant chick silhouette from yellow butcher paper. Then, cut out several large yellow wings, and staple them to the chick. Glue yellow feathers on the top wing. As you discuss and observe new stages of development, use the interactive writing process to write about them on each wing. Reread the wings daily. Glue photos from a book or the Internet on each wing to illustrate the writing.

Materials

- baby chicks
- nonfiction books about chicks
- yellow butcher paper
- scissors
- stapler
- glue
- yellow feathers
- interactive writing materials

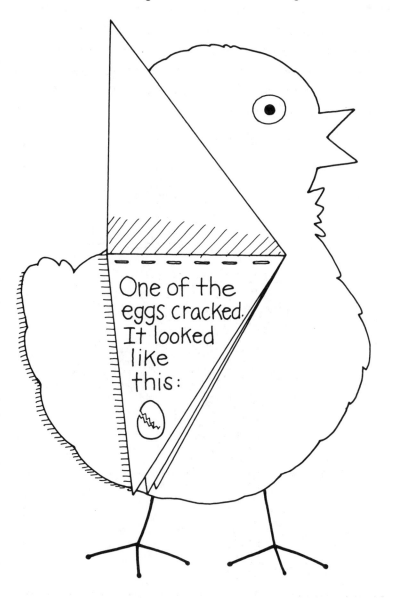

One of the eggs cracked. It looked like this:

Independent Writing

After reading several nonfiction books about chicks, give children the opportunity to create fictional stories that incorporate what they learned about the life cycle of the chicken. Invite children to illustrate the pages, and bind them into a class book for rereading.

Numbers in Our World

Materials

- watercolors/paintbrushes
- construction paper
- scissors
- glue
- butcher paper
- sentence strips
- interactive writing materials

Brainstorm with the class different places in the classroom, at home, and in the world where numbers can be found. Discuss why numbers are so important in these places. Then, invite each child to choose something to watercolor on construction paper that has numbers on it, such as a telephone, a clock, a dog tag, a computer, tickets, or a price tag. Have children cut it out and glue it on a large butcher paper mural. Each day, identify a few of the pictured items and discuss why the numbers are important. Then, use the interactive writing process to have children write on sentence strips a label for each item. Add the labels to the mural.

Independent Writing

Invite each child to continue to explore the importance of numbers in the world on the Investigating Numbers in My Home reproducible (page 90). Have children search for items with numbers and record them on the reproducible.

Math

Adding at the Zoo

Read many books about zoo animals to your class. Review addition skills. Brainstorm with children animals that would be found in a zoo. Then, invite each child to paint pictures of a few zoo animals on construction paper. Have children cut out their pictures and put them into a community pile of animals. Each day, ask children to help you select a handful of the painted animals to use in forming addition equations. If you are focusing on one number family, such as different ways to make 5, then brainstorm the combinations before selecting the animals. Glue the animals to a sheet of construction paper. Each day, use interactive writing to have children write on sentence strips or cash-register tape a number sentence and its matching equation. For example, *I see 2 lions and 3 zebras. 2 + 3 = 5.* Attach the strips above the animals. Display the animals on a bulletin board, or bind them into a book for rereading.

Materials

- books about zoo animals
- tempera paint/paintbrushes
- scissors
- glue
- construction paper
- sentence strips or cash-register tape
- interactive writing materials

I see 1 tiger and 2 elephants. 1+2=3

Independent Writing

Ask each child to write a zoo-themed addition story problem on the Solve My Problem reproducible (page 91). For example, *Zookeeper Shannon can see 2 zebras and 3 tigers. There are 5 animals in all.* Have children trade story problems with a classmate. Invite children to use manipulatives to solve their classmate's story problem. Have children draw a picture and write an equation to show their solution on their partner's paper. Combine the work into a class Zoo Addition book organized by number families.

Let's Have Tea!

Materials

- *Miss Spider's Tea Party* by David Kirk
- tempera paint/paintbrushes
- black butcher paper
- scissors
- glue
- construction paper
- teacup cutouts
- 4 drinks (e.g., apple juice, lemonade, fruit punch, iced tea)
- small paper cups
- small cookies (optional)
- sentence strips
- interactive writing materials

Read aloud *Miss Spider's Tea Party*. Have the class use white tempera paint to create a giant spider web on black butcher paper. (This will be the background for your graph.) Invite children to paint a giant Miss Spider on a separate piece of butcher paper. Invite other children to cut her out and glue her to the center of the web. Have volunteers create and glue on eight construction paper legs. Label four teacup cutouts with the name of the drinks you will serve. On the day of the tea party, reread *Miss Spider's Tea Party*. Then, invite each child to taste each of the four drinks. Remind children to hold out their pinky as they sip their drinks, just for fun. You may even wish to serve some small cookies at the tea party. Have children write their name on a teacup cutout and glue it on the graph to show their favorite drink. Use the interactive writing process to have children record their observations about the graph on sentence strips. For example, *Four children liked the iced tea the best* or *Fruit punch was the class favorite*. Glue the strips to the graph, and display it in the room near several Miss Spider books.

Independent Writing

Now that children have had an opportunity to make a group pictorial graph, they are ready to represent the information on individual bar graphs. Have each child use the information on the giant graph to color in his or her own graph on the Tea Party Graph reproducible (page 92). Ask children to write a sentence about what their graph tells them on the bottom of the page.

Miss Spider, Miss Spider
As nice as can be,
Invited us to try
her tea!
We liked...

Most of us like the fruit punch the best.

Connie
Virginia
Doug
Greg
Mitch
Jack
Sam
Sarah

Dale
Kristine
Ron
Shannon
Kim
Chris

Cody
Bryce

Nick

apple juice   lemonade   iced tea   fruit punch

Royal Bear Day

After the class learns about and explores measurement with rulers, ask children to invite their stuffed bear to a Royal Bear Day celebration. Have children complete the Royal Bear Day Invitation reproducible with the correct information for the celebration, and take it home to their stuffed bear. On Royal Bear Day, supply each child with a sentence strip, scissors, a ruler, and decorative items. Tell children to wrap their sentence strip around their bear's head and cut off the extra. Then, have them use the ruler to measure the length of their strip. Ask children to write the number of inches (or centimeters) on the sentence strip. Invite them to decorate their strip to turn it into a crown. Tell children to be sure to have the number of inches showing on the outside of the crown. When each bear has a crown, ask children to sort the bears by the size of the crowns. Use the interactive writing process to create signs to display next to each group. For example, have children write *Three bears have crowns that are 5 inches long,* and display that sign in front of the three bears on a display table.

Materials

- Royal Bear Day Invitation reproducible (page 93)
- sentence strips
- scissors
- rulers
- decorative items (e.g., beads, sequins, feathers, ricrac, glitter glue)
- interactive writing materials

Shared Writing

Display the bears with their signs in groups, invite children to stand behind their bears, and take their photo. Or, throughout the day, take photos of the children with their "royal" bears doing different activities. Glue the photos to pieces of construction paper, and bind them into a book. During shared writing, discuss the photos and have children write a caption for each page. Reread this book many times for fun memories of Royal Bear Day!

Three bears have crowns that are 5 inches long.

Fraction Fun

Materials

- white and brown construction paper
- scissors
- English muffins
- pizza sauce
- grated cheese
- plastic knives
- toaster oven or microwave
- paper plates or napkins
- stapler
- large pizza box
- interactive writing materials

In advance, prepare at least six white and six brown construction paper pizza shapes. Draw writing lines on the white paper. After introducing the concept of fractions, have each child make a mini-pizza with half of an English muffin, pizza sauce, and cheese. After cooking the pizzas, guide children in a lesson on fractions. As you introduce each fraction, have children divide their pizza into slices of equal size (fourths, eighths, etc.). The following day, review the fractions introduced with the pizzas. Divide the class into small groups, and give each group a brown pizza shape. Give each group a different fraction, and have groups divide their pizza into slices of equal size. Have children draw pizza toppings on some of the slices to show a fractional part of the whole. Show one pizza at a time, and ask children what fraction they see. Use the interactive writing process to have children describe the fraction on the white pizza shapes. For example, *I can see ¼ of a pizza has pepperoni.* Continue using this process until all pizzas have been described. Staple each group's illustrated pizzas to the bottom of a large pizza box, and staple the white pizza shapes inside the top of the box. (Be sure the pizza shapes are stapled at the top only so pages can be flipped up like a book.)

Independent Writing

Have children write the steps for creating their pizza on the Fraction Pizza reproducible (page 94). Invite them to illustrate a fraction on the pizza.

Zero the Hero

In advance, cut out and glue a copy of the Zero the Hero reproducible to six large sheets of construction paper. Divide the class into six groups, and invite them to each color one Zero the Hero. Use the interactive writing process to have children brainstorm and record items that Zero the Hero might see, smell, hear, taste, and touch on his special day (or on the 100th day of school). Create text on each sheet for one of the senses and one sheet for the cover. For example, *He can see 100 ladybugs. He can smell 100 flowers. He can hear 100 bees. He can taste 100 jelly beans. He can touch 100 cotton balls.* Have each group of children cut out 100 paper items, sort them into groups of five or ten, and glue them to their page for repeated counting. Invite children to glue real objects when possible, such as cotton balls in sets of five or ten. Bind the pages into a class book for rereading, or display them on a bulletin board.

Materials
- Zero the Hero reproducible (page 95)
- scissors
- glue
- large sheets of construction paper
- crayons or markers
- interactive writing materials

He can touch 100 cotton balls.

Independent Writing

Ask children to write on a copy of the If I Were Zero the Hero reproducible (page 96) what they would see, smell, hear, taste, and touch if they were Zero the Hero. For example, *If I were Zero the Hero, I would touch 100 slimy frogs.* Encourage children to use descriptive writing. Ask children to share their stories for oral-language practice and reread them to practice independent reading.

Math

Interactive Writing © 2000 Creative Teaching Press

Assessment

Name: _____   Date: _____

- ❏ Correctly grips a marker
- ❏ Uses alphabet chart or other visual information as a support for letter recognition
- ❏ Recognizes and names the uppercase and lowercase letters of the alphabet
- ❏ Forms uppercase and lowercase letters correctly
- ❏ Knows the sound-symbol relationships of most consonants
- ❏ Hears dominant sounds in words
- ❏ Represents sounds heard with letters
- ❏ Sequences sounds heard
- ❏ Claps syllables in words
- ❏ Leaves adequate space between words
- ❏ Uses capitalization correctly
- ❏ Uses punctuation correctly
- ❏ Recognizes the difference between letters and words
- ❏ Indicates the correct number of words in a sentence
- ❏ Uses left-to-right progression and return sweep
- ❏ Tracks text word-by-word while rereading

- ❏ Links words to be written with names of children in the class
- ❏ Knows the sound-symbol relationships of vowels
- ❏ Writes letters unassisted
- ❏ Segments words
- ❏ Writes core high-frequency words
- ❏ Links known words to unknown words
- ❏ Uses familiar chunks to write words (-ed, -ing)
- ❏ Uses reading skills and strategies
- ❏ Writes letters without copying visual information
- ❏ Writes words with little support

	Writes quickly and easily	Needs more practice
Letters		
Words		
Word parts		
Letter-sound relationships		
Spelling patterns		
Strategies used to write new words		

Sequencing Cards

Interactive Writing © 2000 Creative Teaching Press

Porridge Recipe

Three Bears' Porridge

Add 1 cup _____.

Mix with 2 cups _____.

Stir in some _____.

Sprinkle on _____.

Stir and enjoy!

Wolf and Little Red Riding Hood

Interactive Writing © 2000 Creative Teaching Press

Alphabet Bag Note

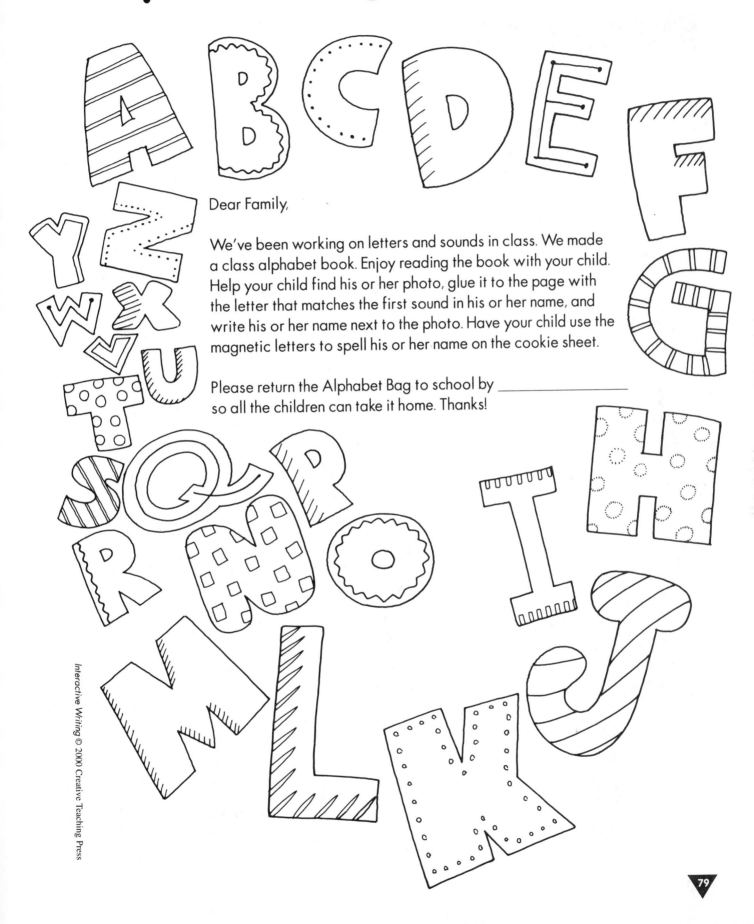

Dear Family,

We've been working on letters and sounds in class. We made a class alphabet book. Enjoy reading the book with your child. Help your child find his or her photo, glue it to the page with the letter that matches the first sound in his or her name, and write his or her name next to the photo. Have your child use the magnetic letters to spell his or her name on the cookie sheet.

Please return the Alphabet Bag to school by _____ so all the children can take it home. Thanks!

Penguin

Name _____

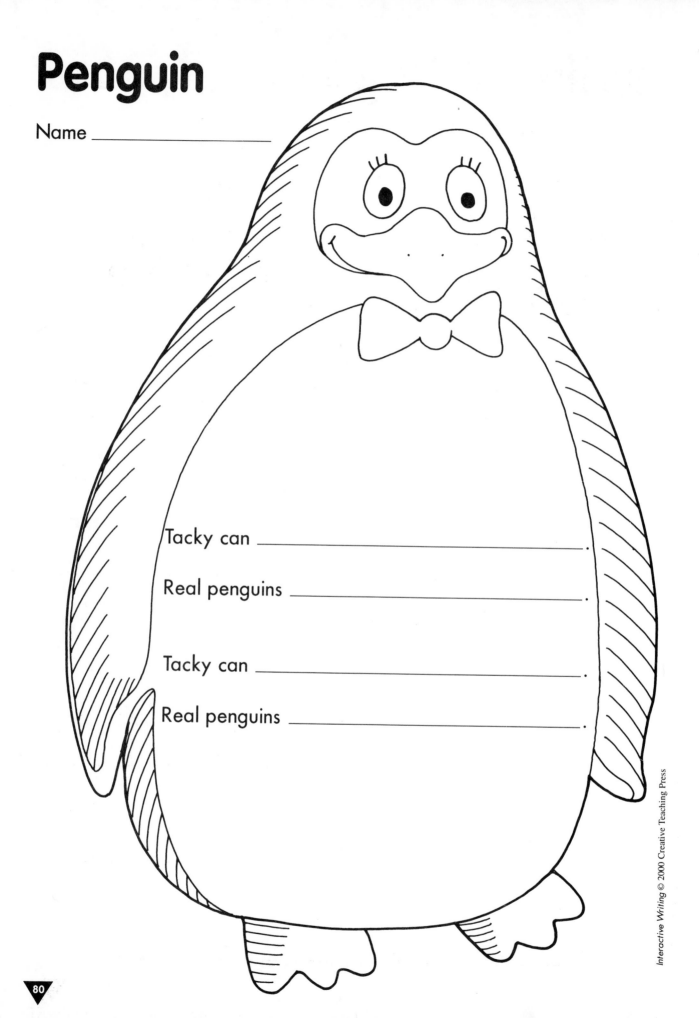

Tacky can _____.

Real penguins _____.

Tacky can _____.

Real penguins _____.

Interactive Writing © 2000 Creative Teaching Press

Turtle

Name _____

Fiction	Fact

Elephant

Letter

Dear _____,

_____

_____

_____

_____

_____

_____

_____

_____

_____

Your friend,

_____

Poetry Pocket

Keep a poem in your pocket!

_____'s

Poetry Pocket

Interactive Writing © 2000 Creative Teaching Press

Diamond Poem

Name _____

On the first row, write the name of a person, place, or thing.

On the second row, write two describing words.

On the third row, write three action words.

On the fourth row, write a synonym for the first word.

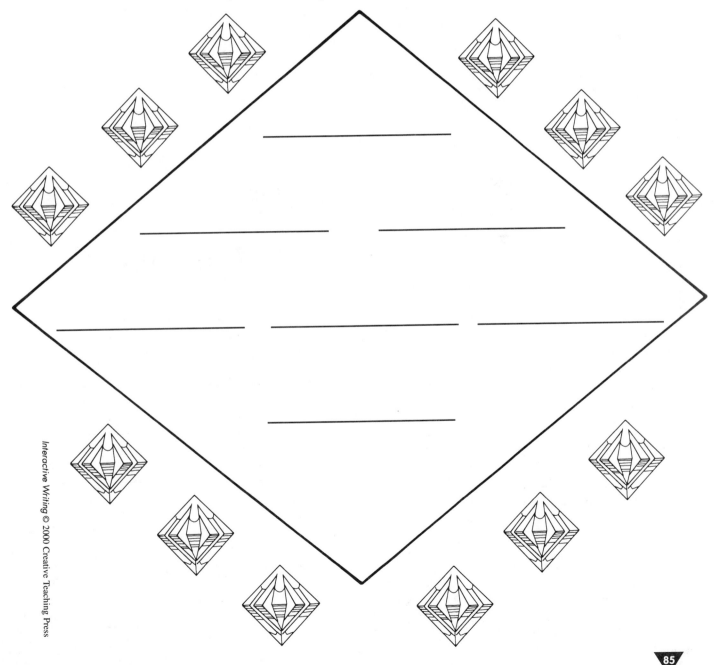

Interactive Writing © 2000 Creative Teaching Press

Passport

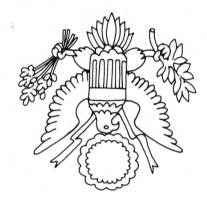

Official

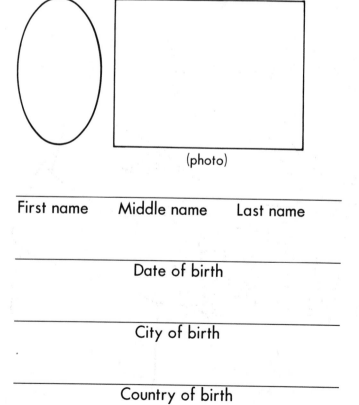

(photo)

First name   Middle name   Last name

Date of birth

City of birth

Country of birth

Destinations

_____

_____

_____

_____

_____

_____

_____

Interactive Writing © 2000 Creative Teaching Press

Parent Letter

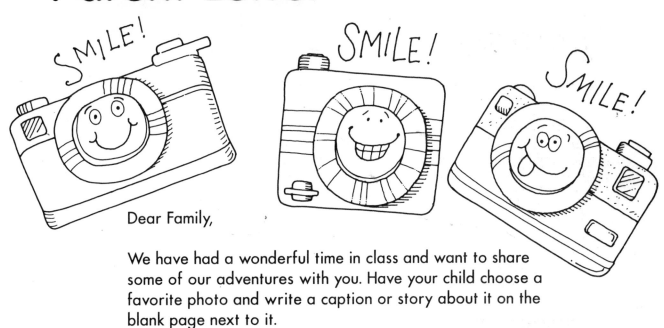

Dear Family,

We have had a wonderful time in class and want to share some of our adventures with you. Have your child choose a favorite photo and write a caption or story about it on the blank page next to it.

Please return the photo book tomorrow so other children may enjoy it!

Thank you,

Pancake

Chef _____'s Pancake Recipe

1. _____

2. _____

3. _____

4. _____

5. _____

My pancake looked like this:

Pancakes, pancakes on the tray.
Children like them long ago and today.

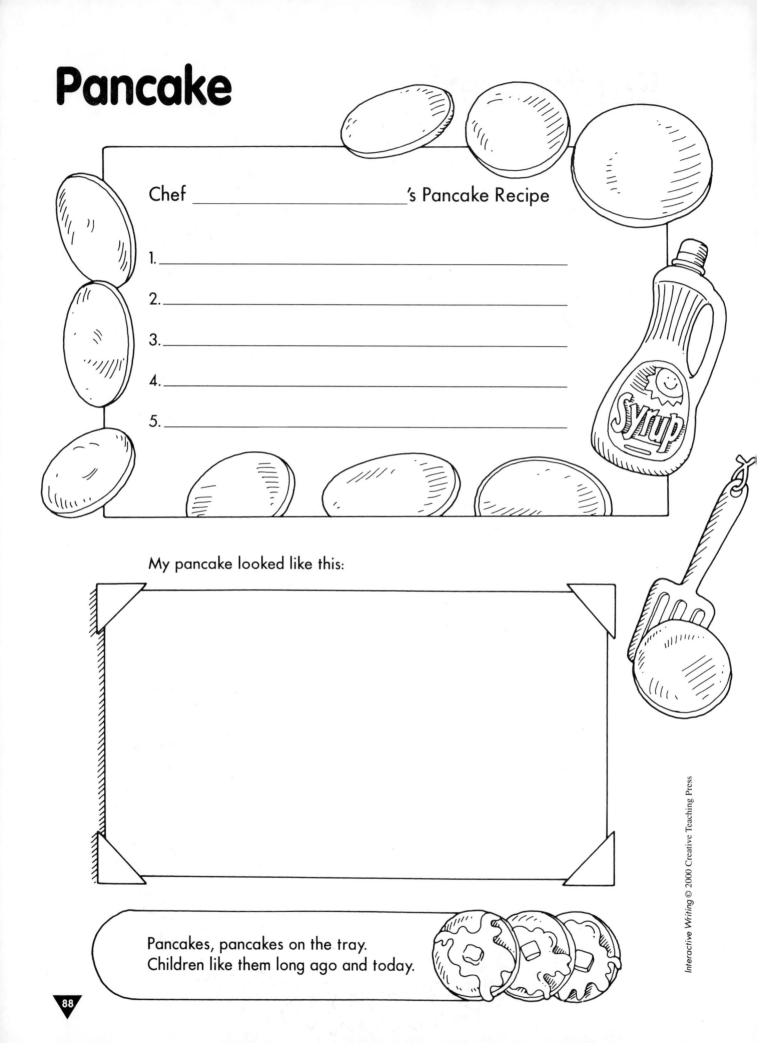

Sunflower

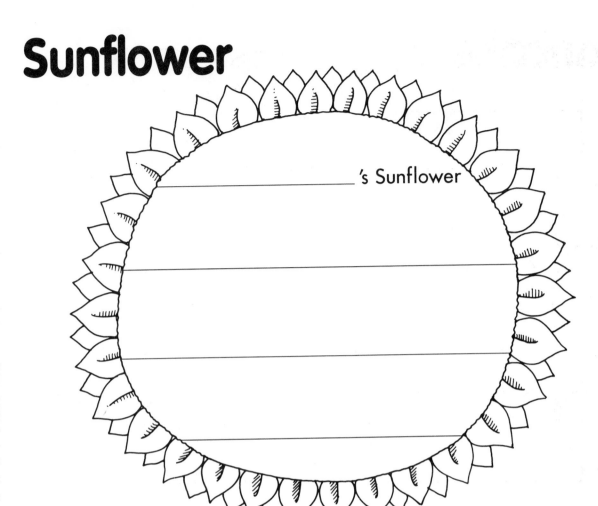

_____ 's Sunflower

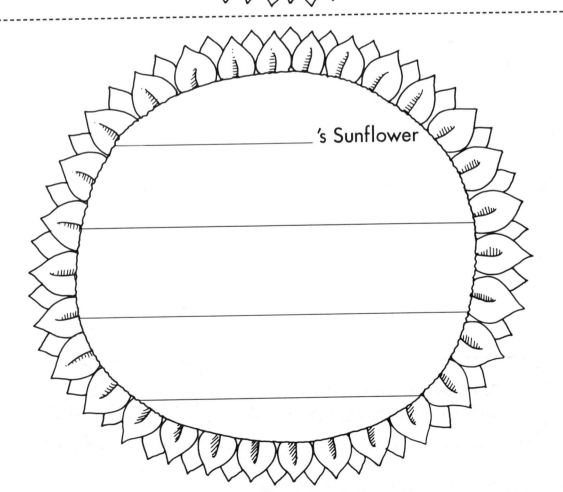

_____ 's Sunflower

Investigating Numbers in My Home

We're learning about the importance of numbers in our world. Please help your investigator find and draw items with numbers in your home. For example, students can look for numbers on a clock, on measuring cups, on a phone, or in their address.

by Investigator _____

I have _____ numbers in my room.

I have _____ numbers in my living room.

I have _____ numbers in my kitchen.

I have _____ numbers in my neighborhood.

Interactive Writing © 2000 Creative Teaching Press

Solve My Problem

Zookeeper _____ can see _____ _____

and _____ _____ . There are _____ animals in all.

Tea Party Graph

by Guest _____

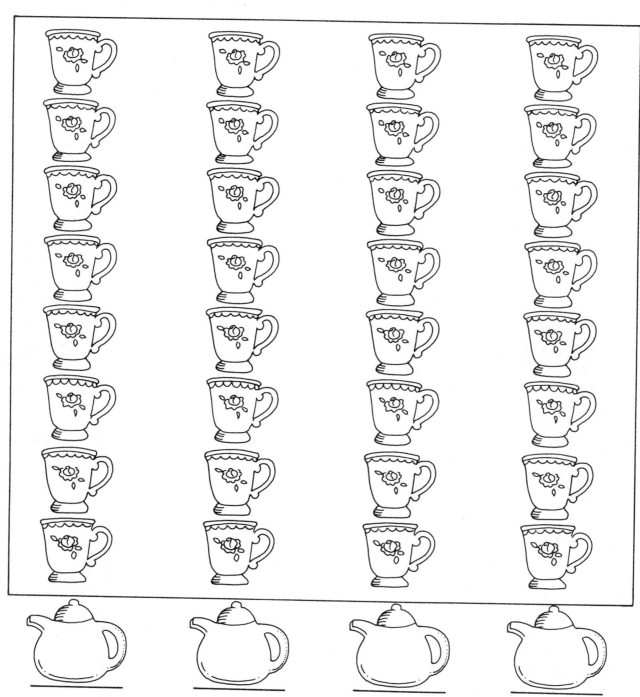

My graph tells me that _____

_____.

Interactive Writing © 2000 Creative Teaching Press

Royal Bear Day Invitation

You are cordially invited to . . .

Our Royal Bear Day celebration!

Who:_____

What:_____

When:_____

Where:_____

Why:_____

Fraction Pizza

Interactive Writing © 2000 Creative Teaching Press

Zero the Hero

Interactive Writing © 2000 Creative Teaching Press

If I Were Zero the Hero

by _____

I would taste _____ .

I would see _____ .

I would smell _____ .

I would touch _____ .

I would hear _____ .

Interactive Writing © 2000 Creative Teaching Press